D0516259

# Pleasant Hill
# SHAKER FURNITURE

# Pleasant Hill
# SHAKER FURNITURE

Kerry Pierce

DRAWINGS BY KEVIN PIERCE
PHOTOGRAPHS BY AL PARRISH

**POPULAR WOODWORKING BOOKS**
CINCINNATI, OHIO
www.popularwoodworking.com

## Read This Important Safety Notice

Distributed in Canada by Fraser Direct
100 Armstrong Avenue
Georgetown, Ontario L7G 5S4
Canada

Distributed in the U.K. and Europe by David & Charles
Brunel House
Newton Abbot
Devon TQ12 4PU
England
Tel: (+44) 1626 323200
Fax: (+44) 1626 323319
E-mail: postmaster@davidandcharles.co.uk

Distributed in Australia by Capricorn Link
P.O. Box 704
Windsor, NSW 2756
Australia

Visit our Web site at www.popularwoodworking.com
for information on more resources for woodworkers.

Other fine Popular Woodworking Books are available
from your local bookstore or direct from the publisher.

11   10   09   08   07      5   4   3   2   1

Library of Congress Cataloging-in-Publication Data

Pierce, Kerry.
   Pleasant Hill Shaker furniture / by Kerry Pierce ; il-
lustrations, Kevin Pierce ; photography, Al Parrish.
-- 1st ed.
       p. cm.
   Includes index.
   ISBN-13: 978-1-55870-795-5 (hardcover : alk. paper)
   ISBN-10: 1-55870-795-6 (hardcover : alk. paper)
   1.  Furniture making. 2.  Shaker furniture. 3.  Shakers--
Kentucky--Pleasant Hill. I. Title.
   TT194P538 2007
   749.088'2898--dc22
                          2006029532
ACQUISITIONS EDITOR: David Thiel
SENIOR EDITOR: Jim Stack
DESIGNER: Brian Roeth
PRODUCTION COORDINATOR: Jennifer Wagner
PHOTOGRAPHER: Al Parrish
ILLUSTRATOR: Kevin Pierce

F+W PUBLICATIONS, INC.

## Metric Conversion Chart

| TO CONVERT | TO | MULTIPLY BY |
|---|---|---|
| Inches | Centimeters | 2.54 |
| Centimeters | Inches | 0.4 |
| Feet | Centimeters | 30.5 |
| Centimeters | Feet | 0.03 |
| Yards | Meters | 0.9 |
| Meters | Yards | 1.1 |

## Acknowledgements

ALL BOOKS ARE JOINT EFFORTS. The author gets to put his or her name on the cover, but the content is never solely the product of that author's efforts. In my career as a writer, this was never so true as it was in the creation of this particular book. Here are the people to whom I owe the most thanks:

First, Chris Schwarz, the editor of *Popular Woodworking* magazine whose idea it was to send me and the magazine's photographer, Al Parrish, to Pleasant Hill in 2005 to do a series of articles about the principles of Shaker design and joinery I saw there. With Chris's kind permission, that initial assignment of two articles grew to five, each of which was published in his magazine over a period of a year and a half. (And thanks, too, to Megan Fitzpatrick, the magazine's managing editor, who was endlessly helpful and kind in the preparation of those articles.)

Second, Jim Stack, who saw in those articles an idea for a book. It was Jim's commitment to this title and his confidence in me that made it happen. I will be forever grateful.

Third, Al Parrish, whose clear and consistent vision about how the images in this book should be shot informs every page. I've been lucky enough to have worked with Al a number of times in the past, and the experience is always a delight. I love to work with people who understand their craft.

Fourth, my brother Kevin (Chuck), who prepared the dozens of extraordinary drawings you see on these pages. For over ten years, he and I have been working together on projects like this, and his illustrations are continually improving. This book, I think, presents his very best work.

Fifth, Dixie Huffman, who has been associated with the restoration of Pleasant Hill for over thirty years. There are literally thousands of pieces of Shaker work on display in the many buildings there, and Dixie knows the whereabouts and history of every single one. Time and again, when I asked her if such-and-such a piece existed, she paused, reflected, and then led me unerringly, without reference to any digitized or hard-copy reference, to the right shelf in the right room of the right building. She is simply amazing.

Sixth, Larrie Curry, the vice president and museum director of Pleasant Hill, who offered me access to her own voluminous knowledge of the Pleasant Hill collection. While Dixie knows the location and history of every individual piece in the Pleasant Hill collection, Larrie is profoundly informed about the big picture. She understands where Pleasant Hill stands in the pantheon of American living museums, and she has a clear vision

of where she would like to guide this incredible facility in the future. Plus, as my deadline drew near, Larrie patiently answered the dozens of questions I directed her way and supplied me with the black-and-white illustrations you see here, which are the property of Shakertown at Pleasant Hill.

Seventh, my family—Elaine, Emily, and Andy—who together comprise the foundation on which my life is built. Without them, nothing would be possible.

Eighth, Cierra Flack, a good friend whose presence in my life enriched it immeasurably.

Despite the fact that Larrie Curry (and her associate Susan Hughes) reviewed the first draft, they did not review the final draft. Any errors in the text, then, should be laid on my doorstep, not theirs.

*Kerry Pierce*

ILLUSTRATING WOODWORKING BOOKS has been both frustrating and rewarding. Not being a woodworker myself, I've found the process of figuring out how to build furniture on paper to be a real challenge. The following people have been very helpful and supportive in this endeavor.

I'd like to thank my brother Kerry who, in spite of my inexperience as a woodworker and as an artist, asked me to illustrate his first book. Even though working with me has frequently challenged his patience, Kerry has continued to ask me to illustrate his books, and has advised me in furniture construction and in illustration. This advice has regularly met resistance, but has almost always been right (please don't tell him).

Jim Stack, at Popular Woodworking books, for continuing to provide these opportunities.

My wife, Molly, my daughter, Ellen, and my son, Will, for encouraging me and putting up with me, especially as deadlines approached, and sometimes as they passed. They are the motivation for every worthwhile thing I do.

My parents, Jim and Sally, who have always supported me. In 1990, they also helped build our house. The plans for this house were drawn by me, with a good deal of help from my Dad. It was Dad's suggestion to Kerry, based on these plans, that got me started in book illustration work.

My mother-in-law Norine Sacksteder, who has inspired me in many ways. Years before I started drawing furniture, she asked me to make some signs for a flower shop she owned. I carefully measured and drew each letter. That technique doesn't produce a very attractive sign, but I felt comfortable using rulers, squares and other tools for drawing, and I still do.

John Kassay, whose *Book of Shaker Furniture* is the best example of measured furniture drawings I've seen. Each of the hundreds of measured drawings I've done have led me at least once to this book.

Miles Overholser, a local sign painter, and an especially talented letterer. After looking over some of my early illustrations, he offered some lettering advice which made a significant difference in the appearance of future projects.

*Kevin Pierce*

# Contents

*Introduction*  10

## Two Journeys  *12*

## Pushing Back the Wilderness at Shawnee Run  *16*

## The Pleasant Hill Woodshops in the 19th Century  *20*

## The Pleasant Hill Woodshop Today  *38*

## Design Features of Pleasant Hill Furniture  *44*

## The Construction of Casework in the Pleasant Hill Collection  *54*

## The Pleasant Hill Collection  *62*

## The Restored Shaker Community at Pleasant Hill  *158*

*Final Thoughts*  170
*Bibliography*  174
*Suppliers*  175
*Index*  176

# Introduction

If you find yourself staying at the restored Shaker Village at Pleasant Hill, Kentucky some summer night, I have a bit of advice: At dawn, after spending the night in a building designed and built and once occupied by the Shakers, walk out onto the lawn. At that moment when the gathering heat of day is burning away the last smoky tendrils of night-time fog, look across the hills surrounding the village. Scan the horizon to the early morning music of birds and distant livestock. If you do this, I think you'll know something about how it must have felt to have awakened there 150 years ago when Pleasant Hill was a thriving community of 500 practicing Shakers.

I know. In each of the last two summers, I did this on three consecutive mornings during visits I made in order to study some of the Shaker furniture in the Pleasant Hill collection.

Of course, the Shakers wouldn't have slept in air conditioned comfort, as I had. And they were more likely to have gone to their early morning job assignments than to have stepped outside at dawn for a quiet, reflective moment alone.

Because I've spent a good part of my life studying and building Shaker furniture, I was susceptible to the power of the moment. I stepped outside and looked and believed.

# Two Journeys

On May 10, 1774, Ann Lee—a disenchanted Anglican looking for a place that would accept her eccentric brand of religiosity—sailed from Manchester, England aboard a leaking tub named the Mariah, bound for New York City. She was accompanied by a tiny band of followers that included her husband, Abraham Standerin, her brother William Lees and the only member of the party who could read and write—James Whittaker—a disciple who ultimately died exhausted by his efforts to spread the Shaker faith in his new country. Once in America, the group briefly separated to find work. Then two years later, they reconvened (minus Ann's husband, who had disappeared, possibly exasperated by his wife's commitment to celibacy) on a leased patch of swampy land more than 100 miles north of the city. They then

went about the business of creating the greatest communal society in American history.

This journey into the wilderness of Upstate New York is well known to students of Shaker history. Less well known, but just as important, is another journey into the wilderness undertaken thirty years later, after the death of Ann Lee, by three sons of the Shaker nation: John Meacham, Issachar Bates and Benjamin Seth Youngs.

This second journey ultimately resulted in the establishment of seven new Shaker communities scattered across the western frontier, among them the community at Pleasant Hill, Kentucky.

### The Missionary Journey

At 3:00 A.M. on January 1, 1805, Meacham, Bates and Youngs left the New Lebanon, New York, headquarters of the Shaker movement and headed for points West. (In the Shaker universe, West referred to those regions between the eastern seaboard and the Mississippi River.) They were dressed in the Shaker fashion of the day in long, black coats, wide-brimmed hats and trousers long enough to cover their shoe tops. They were accompanied by a packhorse loaded with the supplies they would need for a journey that might last months, if not years, and $535 in cash. They also carried a letter from the New Lebanon ministry in support of their missionary efforts.

This proselytizing journey was not the first in the brief history of Ann Lee's movement. In May of 1781, she had herself traveled from New York State into neighboring states, spreading her message, and—despite the persecution of some New Englanders who felt threatened by that message—the earlier missionary journey had resulted in the establishment of several important Shaker communities.

The three missionaries sent to the West were well chosen. John Meacham was the son of Joseph Meacham who had been one of Ann Lee's first American converts and subsequently her right-hand man. In fact, it had been Joseph, along with Lucy Wright, who had taken charge of the movement after Lee's death, providing structure and order to the first Shaker communities. Issachar Bates proved to be such a charismatic speaker that Barton Stone—a Kentucky minister among the first to hear the Shaker message brought West by the missionaries—said about his reaction to Bates that he (Stone) "...was never so completely swallowed up by any man as with Issacher Bates". Bates was well known for this oratorical power. F. Gerald Ham, an important figure in the world of Pleasant Hill scholarship, described Bates as "...a man consumed with a passion to spread the Shaker faith to the edge of the American frontier...a modern day Saint Paul". And Benjamin Seth Youngs was perhaps the ablest member of this trio. He was the Shaker scholar who later codified the Christian faith as it was interpreted by Ann Lee and her followers in a version of the Bible—*The Testimony of Christ's Second Appearing*—originally published in 1808 at Lebanon, Ohio. And it was Youngs who in August of 1805 was entrusted with the responsibility of presenting the doctrine of Ann Lee to the early religious leaders in central Kentucky.

For two months, the three missionaries traveled in the general direction of the western frontier, moving on through January and February, driven by the power of their faith, as they negotiated both winter weather and the often poorly maintained dirt roads.

At first, they headed south by carriage to Peekskill, New York. Then on foot, leading their packhorse, they continued on to New York City, crossing the Hudson River into New Jersey, where they pushed to the western border of the state. They passed next through Delaware and Maryland, working their way around the upper

reaches of the Chesapeake Bay.

They then moved westward up into the Appalachian Mountains, a protracted ascent which must have taxed even their travel-hardened bodies. They crossed the Shenandoah River and headed generally southwest paralleling the Appalachian spine, crossing finally into Tennessee and on into Kentucky, 1200 miles distant from their starting point at New Lebanon, New York.

As planned, the three missionaries arrived on the frontier at an opportune moment: on the heels of several regional religious revivals, including the New Light revival. Many of those who had taken part in these revivals included, in their religious practices, physical gyrations similar to those that had given the Shakers their common name.

On March 13, 1805, the missionaries arrived at Cane Ridge, Kentucky, which had been the site four

years earlier of the great Cane Ridge Revival, during which an estimated 20,000 people expressed themselves in five days and four nights of riotous, ground-shaking, hell-raising worship. Robert W. Finley, a local minister who had attended the Revival, described a Dante-esque scene of "…fires reflecting light amidst the swaying branches of the trees, the hundreds of persons moving to and fro,—singing, praying, shouting from different parts of the (Cane Ridge) grounds like the sounds of many rushing rivers…. Such as tried to escape conviction by leaving were frequently struck down upon the way and compelled to return of their own accord." This revival included among its expressions of religious fervor even "jerking, rolling, running, dancing and barking".

The leadership at New Lebanon had chosen wisely. This fertile Kentucky soil had been carefully prepared to accept the seed of impassioned Shaker religiosity.

# Pushing Back the Wilderness at Shawnee Run

The three missionaries spoke to the citizens of Cane Ridge, including Reverend Barton Stone, about the tenets of the Shaker faith, including the equality of the sexes, the communal ownership of goods, celibacy and the second appearance of Christ in the person of Ann Lee. Bates later wrote of this visit that "...the people sucked in our light as greedily as ever an ox drank water..."

The Shaker missionaries then went from one frontier outpost to another, moving across Kentucky, up into Ohio, then back again, seeking out local leaders of the New Light Revival movement, working to convert them to the missionaries' own brand of revivalism.

Finally, on August 16, 1805, Benjamin Seth Youngs,

in the company of three recently converted members of one of the indigenous revival movements visiting from Ohio, offered his testimony to three Kentucky men who would later become important figures in the Pleasant Hill community: Samuel and John Banta and Elisha Thomas. Youngs must have been incredibly persuasive because on that day—a scant five months after the arrival of the three missionaries from New Lebanon—Elisha Thomas accepted the Shaker faith.

It would be difficult to overstate the magnitude of the missionaries' accomplishment in salesmanship. While the New Light movement had paved the way for religious extremism in Kentucky, particularly as that extremism might have expressed itself in vigorous dancing, two of the key elements of the Shaker faith—celibacy and the elevation of women—were contrary to the rough-and-tumble, male-dominated frontier lifestyle that characterized the Kentucky highlands in the opening decade of the 19th century. Women were not seen as chattel, but in a time and place in which physical strength was essential for wresting a living from the land, the superiority of men was simply understood. Plus, in a culture in which the life expectancy was half what it is today, children, the products of sexual union, were essential elements of any farmer's or stockman's long-range plans. Somehow, Benjamin Youngs had managed to convince this Kentucky farmer that what he had probably heretofore believed to be good and true

about the primacy of males and the cultural necessity of sexual union was no longer so.

And the conversion of Elisha Thomas was just the beginning. His acceptance of the Shaker faith was quickly followed by the conversion of many of his Kentucky neighbors with the result that two Kentucky Shaker communities were established at South Union and Pleasant Hill in remarkably quick fashion .

The Pleasant Hill location was designated as the site of a new Shaker community for a number of reasons. First, it was on the direct route connecting the rapidly growing city of Lexington and the older, but still important, frontier town of Harrodsburg, Kentucky. There was also access by water via the Kentucky River which ran nearby. Plus, the soil of the Kentucky plateau was fertile even if rocky, and offered sources of timber and Kentucky limestone close at hand. Finally, it was the site of Elisha Thomas's 140 acre holding, a property which would become the core of the Pleasant Hill community, to which many other parcels of land would be added over the next two decades.

In December 1807, Lucy Wright, Ann Lee's successor as leader of the Shaker nation, received an account of the status of the West communities that included this description of the fledgling Pleasant Hill village: "The spot we live is not quite so even as we could wish, yet it is not mountainous like New Lebanon. There is no mountain in sight and the soil is rich and fertile. We are situated on a river by the name of Kentucky River which a considerable part of the year is navigable for boats for about one hundred and forty or fifty miles from its mouth where it empties into the Ohio. The Believers' land is bounded by it on the east, our house stands about three quarters of a mile from it. Up this river there is a number of inexhaustible banks of stone coal, the same with sea coal, which they bring down in boats for black-smithing and other uses."

In 1808, just three years after the departure of the missionaries from New Lebanon, the main avenue of the Pleasant Hill community was laid out in very nearly the same configuration in which it exists today. Then on June 2, 1814, 128 believers signed a covenant requir-ing those Believers to surrender all their worldly goods

to the order, thus marking the official beginning of the Pleasant Hill experiment in communal living. By 1820, Pleasant Hill had grown to over 4,000 acres and almost 500 inhabitants.

There is much to respect about what those first Shakers accomplished at Pleasant Hill. They trans-formed a rocky Kentucky plateau into a community that boasted some of the largest and most magnificent build-ings west of the Appalachians, and they did it without access to the special tooling and special skills available to architects and builders of the period on the eastern seaboard. In the spring of 1805, there was nothing on that plateau but a few simple structures like the rough cabin of Elisha Thomas. Then within thirty years, that setting was almost magically transformed into a beauti-ful and prosperous community of limestone, brick and clapboard.

# The Pleasant Hill Woodshops in the 19th Century

ood was, of course, a primary structural material in all of the Pleasant Hill buildings. Even in the case of structures like the Centre Family Dwelling , with walls laid up of limestone, the beams, joists and rafters that supported the floors, ceilings and roofs were made of wood components pegged or nailed together.

Once a building's shell was completed, the work of joiners and finish carpenters (often the same Shak-

ers who erected the shells) began. Thousands of feet of flooring were sawn out, surfaced, cut to length and fit into place. In some cases, the floorings' edges were treated with plank planes to create tongue-and-groove joints to keep unruly boards from rising out of place.

While this construction was taking place, sash makers and joiners were hard at work making and assembling the many complicated parts required for doors and windows. Sometimes this work would have been accomplished in Pleasant Hill workshops, but it's

likely that then—as now—craftsmen would have set up temporary woodshops within the structures being erected. Next, these elements were installed in the buildings, along with built-in shelves and cupboards which had also been assembled in the woodshops.

In the months during which the shells were being erected and fitted with doors and windows, other craftsmen were thicknessing, ripping out, surfacing and, in some cases, adding molded edges to the hundreds of feet of baseboard, chair rail, peg rail and window casing the buildings required.

In addition to their considerable importance in support of the building trades, woodshops impacted the lives of 19th-century Pleasant Hill Shakers in ways not often seen today. In the 19th century, goods and passengers were transported in wagons and carriages made of wood, fitted with wheels made of wood. Wood was used as packaging (in the creation of wood packaging the Shakers excelled) to store foodstuffs, seeds, clothing and other household goods. The ubiquitous Shaker oval box is a storage concept designed for such applications. Shoemakers sewed shoes on wooden forms. They assembled shoes with pegs split from blocks of wood. And the simple act of transporting fire from one place in the home to another was often accomplished with a tightly wound wooden shaving known as a spill, created with a woodshop tool known as a spill plane. All of these familiar objects were products of Shaker woodshops.

## Materials

The forests surrounding Pleasant Hill offered, close at hand, a generous supply of hardwoods in a wide variety of species, many of which found their way into the Pleasant Hill woodshops.

Cherry was the material of choice for Pleasant Hill casework. This moderately hard species performs well under edge tools, and although it is a bit fragile for load-bearing applications like chairmaking, it is revered for its figure and its photo-reactivity, which results in a gradual and very appealing deepening of its red color over time. Many Pleasant Hill cupboards and chests of drawers intended for offices and living quarters are made of this material. A relatively rare curly variant of this species was used for the secretary (page 80) now housed upstairs in the Meeting House. Walnut was

Cherry was the material of choice for Pleasant Hill casework.

also used for fine furniture, although its relative rarity in Pleasant Hill pieces suggests that it was either not as commonly found as cherry or not as highly prized. The little "Saturday" table (page 72) also housed upstairs in the Meeting House was made of this material.

Poplar was preferred for utilitarian furniture intended to be used in kitchens or workrooms. Poplar is much softer than either cherry or walnut and can be, therefore, more easily nailed, even when relatively dry (all hardwoods can be nailed when they're worked green). Much Pleasant Hill poplar furniture is, in fact, nailed together, like the hanging cupboard on page 94.

Pleasant Hill chairmakers, like those in the World and those in other Shaker communities, employed a variety of materials, often within the same chair, matching each species to specific chairmaking applications. Posts were frequently turned from hard maple, which combines great strength and a uniform density, which holds up well in the turned details of finials and vases under arms. Rungs were frequently made of oak, ash and hickory, the three species being used interchangeably, sometimes within the same chair. These species were, and still are, preferred for rungs because all three offer enormous strength and flexibility even when worked to rather frail-appearing diameters. Slats were often made of these same three species for the same reason.

Pleasant Hill makers did use hardware produced in the World. In fact, it seems that every Pleasant Hill chest and cupboard that could have been locked now sports either a metal lock or the mortise that once housed one. But like Shaker craftsmen in other communities, Pleasant Hill makers often turned their own knobs from wood, typically making them from the same species as the object to which they were applied.

**LEFT** These two well-worn wooden plank planes might have been used to cut tongue and groove joinery on floor boards. The plane on the left cuts the groove, while the plane on the right cuts the tongue that will fit into that groove.

(PHOTO: KERRY PIERCE)

## Tools

Very few of the tools once used in Pleasant Hill woodshops have survived to the present day. Among those that have survived are a handful of woodworking planes.

The most provocative of these is a thin round stamped with the name "Banty" which is a variant of "Banta". Pleasant Hill tradition has associated this plane with Cornelius Banta who was one of the community's first Shaker converts and who did in fact practice woodworking there. Banta died in 1816, and the flat narrow chamfers and the sleeper style finial of the plane's wedge are consistent with a plane of that period.

Despite the lack of surviving Pleasant Hill tools, as a result of the patient compilation of entries from Pleasant Hill family journals, in particular A Temporal Journal Kept by order of the Deacon of the East House, Book B (the Journal), we do know something about the tools used in the woodshops. (The staff at Pleasant Hill did this compilation.)

Francis Montfort, one of the most prolific of known Pleasant Hill woodworking craftsmen, built a "turning

**ABOVE** The Banta molder is the second plane from the left: All four planes have a solid Pleasant Hill provenance. The plane on the extreme left is a simple grooving plane used for cutting the grooved component in a tongue-and-groove joint. The plane next to it is the Banta round. (A round is an unfenced molding plane with a rounded sole that cuts a shallow flute.) A second and wider, round sits behind the Banta plane. The plane at the rear is an adjustable sash plane used for fabricating window sash components. Note the boxing in the sash plane. ("Boxing" is the name to given to the bits of boxwood fitted into the sole of the plane to protect areas prone to heavy wear These are visible as areas of lighter color on the front end of the sash plane.) The complicated boxing would have made this a relatively expensive tool to purchase.

(PHOTO: KERRY PIERCE)

lathe for himself" in 1846, and in 1851 he built "1 jointer for himself". The lathe was likely a treadle lathe, perhaps like the reproduction treadle lathe now being used in the woodworking shop. The jointer would have been a jointing plane, which is a plane with a sole more than 20" in length.

In 1847, Stephen Manire, who was thirteen years older than Montfort but whose time in the Pleasant Hill workshop overlapped the younger man's, built a "table for his shop". We don't know anything more about this piece of furniture, but it does sound as if it might have been a workbench. In fact, given the timing, it might have been the bench on which Montfort worked the hardwood blank from which he fabricated his jointing plane.

Stephen Leonidas Boisseau, who was much younger than either Manire or Montfort but whose time in the workshop also lapped theirs in "June 1847 completed his turning lathe which is set up in the brick shop". This, too, was probably a treadle lathe, although spring-pole lathes were still fairly common in the 19th century.

**BELOW** This nearly unused panel raising plane has a solid Pleasant Hill provenance, but it unfortunately bears no maker's mark. While it is very well made—note the finely crafted tote and the nicely shaped strike button—several details suggest an amateur hand. First the wedge was not given the radiused or beveled corners we see in professionally made planes (although this could be a replacement wedge). Also, the plane lacks "eyes". These extra bevels just ahead of the wedge are probably unnecessary and often left out by amateurs, almost never by professionals.

(PHOTO: KERRY PIERCE)

**DETAIL** Like many panel raisers, this plane has and integral fence (the projection on the lower right of the plane's sole ). Planes of this type cut a beveled field around a panel's central reservation. Some panel raisers cut simple bevels. Others, like this example, cut a field with a fairly complex profile.

**ABOVE** This collection of antique woodworking planes is housed in the current woodshop, although the planes are not used there.

**LEFT** This arrangement of items on a bench in the woodshop is much like one that might have been seen there 150 years ago. Working clockwise from the lower left, you can see a pair of wrought iron bench holdfasts. These pass through holes drilled in the bench surface. When the curved top of the holdfast is tapped, it wedges itself into the hole, pinning the workpiece under the flattened foot of the holdfast to the bench top. A pattern for a clothes hanger is just above the holdfast. A window stay is next. This is designed to hold the lower sash open to allow air flow into the room. A pattern for an oval box body band is next. Several oval box forms stand at 11:00. A pair of clothespins is positioned at high noon. On the extreme right is a form used to shape the straw hats worn by Shaker workmen.

**LEFT** Mark Ross, a costumed interpreter who demonstrates woodworking techniques, uses a drawknife on work held in place by the head of a shaving horse. The work is held in place by the action of the user's feet, freeing both hands for the drawknife.

**BELOW RIGHT** These are examples of some of the coopered work being done today in the Pleasant Hill woodshop.

**BELOW LEFT** The stacked molds on the left are used in the woodshop to create reproduction oval boxes.

## The Work

There is no evidence that the work produced in Pleasant Hill woodshops became an important source of revenue for the community in the way that the work of the New Lebanon chairmaking shop under the direction of Robert Wagan became an important revenue source for that community, although Pleasant Hill records do note an occasional sale of woodwork to the World. Instead, the output of Pleasant Hill woodshops was intended almost entirely for the use of the members of the community.

But that does not mean, however, that the output of those shops was meager. The Journal lists over 120 chairs made by Francis Montfort, and in 1857 and 1858, the Journal notes over 1,000 seed boxes made by that same man. In addition, records indicate that Montfort made thousands of other wooden geegaws for the Pleasant Hill community: "1 beehive", "12 bee benches" (?), "21 bobbins", "1 cupboard for cellar", "2 bonnet boxes", "14 feather brushes", "226 small sundrys", "EF (East Family) candle stand" and on and on.

This meticulous monitoring of woodshop output is a very Shaker concept, one mandated by the leadership, but it's instructive I think to consider the psychology of Francis Monfort and his peers in the Pleasant Hill woodshops as they recorded their accomplishments (this recording was something, presumably, they did themselves). What was Montfort thinking when he noted that he had made "256 fan handles"? Was he thinking, as I might have been: "I turned 256, a new Pleasant Hill record"?

## The Craftsmen

The brief biographies that follow are based on the work of the Pleasant Hill staff that assembled an enormous amount of information taken from the family journals.

This molding plane, a thin round, is stamped with the name Banty, a variant of Banta. Pleasant Hill tradition associates this plane with Cornelius Banta.

My list of biographies does not include every person known to have worked in a woodshop. Instead, I chose what I think are representative biographies that together I hope will offer a glimpse into the lives of the Pleasant Hill woodworking craftsmen.

**Cornelius Banta** was born perhaps in 1781 in Mercer County, Kentucky. Banta was one of the Shawnee Run (later renamed Pleasant Hill) converts to whom Benjamin Seth Youngs assigned duties in the earliest years of the Kentucky Shaker experience: "...and Cornelius Banta and Joe(l) Shields to work in the joiner shop." Banta signed the Covenant—a contract to accept all the principles of the Shaker faith—when the church was first organized in June of 1814. His trade was listed alternately as furniture maker, stockman, cooper. He died of consumption in 1816 at age 35.

**Stephen Leonidas Boisseau** was born in East Baton Rouge, Louisiana, on June 1, 1821. He signed the Covenant on November 18, 1842. Boisseau is one of those craftsmen whose biography illustrates the many hats Shaker workmen were expected to wear. Pleasant Hill records indicate he was carpenter, a commercial agent (for dealing with the World), a peddler, a teacher, a boys caretaker, an Elder (a position of leadership within the Shaker community) and a furniture maker.

The Journal records several bedsteads he made. In addition, in June 1847, the Journal notes that Boisseau "...completed his turning lathe which he set up in the brick shop." But the most interesting Journal notes regarding Boisseau are those identifying simple machines he constructed. He "...made a crane for the nurses room to raise Sally Hooser in and out of bed". He also made a "...crane for the East Wash House". In 1858, the Journal notes that he made a "...windless for ice house, and windless for well". (Presumably, these last notations refer to the machine we identify as a "windlass", that is a crank on which rope can be wrapped or unwrapped to raise or lower an object suspended from the rope.) Boisseau died after a brief illness in 1894.

**Josephus J. Curtis** was born July 14, 1825 in Mercer County, Kentucky. He signed the Covenant on November 13, 1847. Curtis, listed as a woodturner, stayed at Pleasant Hill for only a few years, but his story is typical of the stories of many who came into the community quite young, and then, instead of integrating seamlessly into Pleasant Hill as adult Shakers, behaved badly and left. Records describe an encounter between young Curtis and Elder Benjamin Dunlavy this way: "Josephus Curtis with a brutality that would...almost have disgraced a canibal (sic) struck his own Elder while making labours with him; soon afterwards went to the World/ 5-20-48 came in company of bro. James Curtis to get his clothes, did not act amiss but went away friendly/".

# January 1st 1870.

1-1 Copter—Salvaging Ministry—100. East 80. West 70. N. F. 29. W. S. 263. 342.

1. The Year Commences with 342 Souls in Society.
Rain, this morning, but the day closed with snow.
Move—John Pilkington from the North to Centre Family.
Also—A boy, Frederic Houston from same to West Family.

2. Snow—Blowing, blustering—7 inches deep & terribly drifted.

3. Mercury—This morning 16° above Zero.—

6. After Wood—Stephen Boisseau, went with some hands
to take an empty Coal Boat to Boman's Bottom for wood.
A Steam Boat Started with it but left it in the reffle &
The Company took it up by hand—loaded & brot it down
The following day.—

7. Absconded—George Earls from West Family again. see
Also—J R Bryant to Lexington returned next day.

8. Regulators—Passed here westward last night or half-
past 8. Called at the Office, said the threat about the
Negroes was bogus—We need not heed it but hire whom
we pleased & we should be protected—They returned
about 11. P.M. got Supper at the North Family & then
departed.—Cold Mercury at 10° this morning.

9. Mercury at 0. Zero, the first time this winter.—

10. Ice getting—Mercury at 16° commenced getting Ice,
it became brittle in the afternoon—Tightened up by next
morning when we finished.—

13. Change of Tenants—James Richardson & family, vacated
the House at the grist Mill—Floyd Burks occupies &
takes charge of The Mill.—

16. Return from Orleans—Elkanah Scott & J. Burnett.
having left here the 23rd of November last.—

17. Rain Thunder & Lightning last night 1½ inches fell
from Noon yesterday to Noon to day.—

18. Return—Br Jacob Kulp from Arkansas, sold seeds & presents.

**Leander Gettys** was born in Pittsburgh, Pennsylvania on Christmas Day in 1832. He signed the Covenant on May 10, 1856. Gettys career as a furniture maker is distinguished by the fact that there are more pieces signed by him than by any other Pleasant Hill craftsman, including a table that appears in this book. The Pleasant Hill collection includes two tables and a candlebox bearing his name. Like Josephus Curtis in the above entry, Gettys' life as a Shaker ended ignominiously. Pleasant Hill records contain this description of Gettys' final moments as a Shaker: " 11-2-65: ... A. Kulp & Leander Gettys went to Lexington & Abraham returned, but Leander took the other road and ingloriously fled." A later notation contains this follow-up: "Leander Gettys had the effrontery to come here on a visit."

**Alexander Milligan** was born July 8, 1849. He signed the Covenant on October 6, 1868. Milligan's story represents the membership crisis that threatened every Shaker community in the country during the latter half of the 19th century. Whereas the physical comfort and security of a Shaker life was attractive in the brutal early decades of the 19th century, the country's growing prosperity in the years after the Civil War offered new options to people in the lower economic classes. The industrialization of America made jobs available to almost anyone who wanted to work, and so people who might once have become Shakers in order to dine at bountiful Shaker tables could now choose to work in factories and then enjoy their private lives as they saw fit.

Milligan's troubled relationship with the Pleasant Hill lifestyle began even before he signed the Covenant, as this notation from July 9, 1862, illustrates: "David Milligan absconded from the Center Family, and Richard and Alexander Milligan & Mary Clark, sister to the Milligans from the East Family, and Eliza Kid from the West F. (Family). A budget of hypocrisy!" Later, there is this notation, which reflects not only the Shaker willingness to forgive wayward members, but their need to do anything they could to maintain their rapidly dwindling membership: "March 10, 1868 Alexander Milligan returned and readmitted to EF (East Family)". But his second stay at Pleasant Hill was not a long one. Records later indicate that before his death in 1915, Milligan had worked for 20 years as a cabinetmaking instructor at the University of Kentucky. When he died—as a result of burns he received from a fire in his shop—he left behind a wife, two sons and a daughter.

**Francis Montfort** was born May 3, 1784. He was one of the original signers of the Pleasant Hill covenant on June 2, 1814. He is listed in Pleasant Hill records variously as a gardener, mechanic, furniture maker and tool maker.

Monfort appears to have been a gifted woodworker, knowledgeable about many branches of the craft. The Journal records some of his enormous output. He made, for example, a significant number of chairs. The Journal notes that Montfort made "2 chair frames EF (East Family)", "4 common (side chair) frames CF (Centre Family)", "1 arm chair", "4 chairs for Office & 1 for sale", "2 arm chairs for CF", "26 chairs for EF" and so on.

The Journal notes a number of case pieces as well: "1 trunk, 3 sinks (dry sinks?) for EF", "2 wood boxes for EF", "ash hopper", "1 pie safe", "for EF 4 wood boxes".

Further, Montfort made all manner of mechanical contraptions. He built a "turning lathe for himself (he probably wore out several)", "machine for rolling pie crust", "2 ginnies (spinning jennies?)", "potato masher for CF", "1 shoe press" and "1 fat press".

And he produced a simply astonishing amount of incidental wooden items: "19 clothes pin", "42 sm. Broom handles", " 15 clothes pins", "49 spools", "48 fan handles", "501 seed boxes", "571 seed boxes", "459 basket ribs", and another notation for "584 basket ribs".

I should mention here that the above paragraphs represent only a tiny fraction of the work attributed to Francis Montfort.

As if this weren't enough, the Journal also records hundreds of items he repaired in his shop. He died in 1867.

**William F. Pennebaker**, who was nominally a cabinetmaker, was born on August 2, 1841, signing the Covenant on October 6, 1868. Pennebaker's story illustrates another problem the Shakers faced late in the 19th century. Whereas in the early years, the Pleasant Hill Shakers were largely self-sufficient, teaching themselves, when necessary, to be stone masons, brick makers, plumbers, machinists, agronomists and so on, in the later years, they needed to look outside the Pleasant Hill community for necessary training. This was due in part because of the accumulation of deaths within the Pleasant Hill leadership in the later years of the 19th century. But also, the world outside Pleasant Hill was changing, and in order to keep pace with the breakthroughs in science and technology occurring there, it was necessary to send Shakers out into the World to receive training.

Pennebaker was one of those Shakers who went out into the World. The Pleasant Hill Community sent him into the World (to Cincinnati according to Pleasant Hill tradition) to be trained in general medicine and surgery, after which he returned to Pleasant Hill.

When he died in 1922, his obituary described him as "...a man of courtly & polished manners, genial...one of the widest read and best informed men in Mercer Co."

This photo from the late 1880s shows a group of West Family Shakers on the steps of the West Family Dwelling. Dr. Francis Pennebaker (1837-1902), a dentist, stands at the rear. He came to Pleasant Hill as a boy in 1849. Sarah Pennebaker (1839-1916) is the Sister in the chair on the left. Mary Constant (?) is the Sister holding the cat. Mary Pettus, who arrived at Pleasant Hill in May of 1883, is sitting on the top left step. Lula Harris, who arrived at Pleasant Hill in 1882 at age 14, is seated in the middle right. Below her is Cynthia Shain (1827-1906), who was brought to Pleasant Hill by her uncle in 1843.

(PHOTO BY J. L. S.)

# December 24th 1870.

**24.** Extreme Cold — Mercury this Morning 8° below Zero! —

Ice getting — We commenced getting Ice it being about 4 inches thick on an average — We drew it up from the pond on an inclined rail way, which did good business. It was commenced last year very temporarily — Improved this year, & promises to be valuable — It was invented by William & Francis Pennebaker —

**25** Christmas — Mercury at Zero — being Sabbath & kept as such — Meetings as usual —

**26** Mercury 28° above Zero. Finished Ice getting it being Full 5 inches thick — see 24th Inst.

**27** Move Children — Maggie & Kate Richardson from the North family to the Centre — Mer. 14° above Zero.

**28** Broom trip — S. L. Boisseau & hired teamster went to Lexington with Brooms & returned the following day. —

**29** Mercury. 18° above Zero — & 30. Mer 30° above 0. —

**31** Pleasant — Summary of improvements the past year are

1st An addition to the East end of the West Familys Barn & Wing south —

2nd Centre Wagon shop repaired by rebuilding the Stone & brick work of the West side & the brick work of the South end —

3d Building — A small frame erected for store house at Shaker landing on the River — & New Scales put up over the River —

4. Rebuilding Arches in all the Wash Houses in the Church — H. Daily & F Pennebaker performed the Work — Eld B. B. Dunlavy & J Shelton assisted with those at the Centre — Thus ends another year of Labor & toil — So. Ends.

1870.

James Shelton, the Pleasant Hill miller, stands in the door of the Centre Family Dwelling.

(PHOTO BY J. L. S.)

**RIGHT** Dr. William Pennebaker, in an effort to reinvigorate the Pleasant Hill workshops, decided to attempt making "staveless" woodenware by turning vessels from blocks of solid wood, rather than assembling them from individual staves (vertical segments). This lathe was apparently set up to perform this work, although there is no evidence the efforts ever paid off. (Circa 1880)

**BELOW** Here a group of Shakers poses for the camera, probably during a day of "releasement" sometime in the latter part of the 19th century. A "releasement" was an excursion away from the daily grind of Shaker life, often taking the form of a walk along the Kentucky River.

**RIGHT** This photo from the late 1890s shows Sister Cynthia Shain feeding ducks. Notice the disrepair of the farm buildings in the background. By the time this photo was taken, the Pleasant Hill community was little more than a shadow of its earlier vibrancy and power.

BELOW   A group of Shakers makes con-
versation at a Pleasant Hill grist mill.
(circa 1887)
(PHOTO BY MONTGOMERY H. ROCHESTER)

**ABOVE** Pleasant Hill Shakers, like those of other communities, sold the products of their workshops and fields to the World. In this early photo, a group of people from the World poses with Shaker Brethren outside the Pleasant Hill broom shop. The restored Pleasant Hill community today maintains a small broom-making operation, using the same tools as the 19th-century Pleasant Hill Shakers. The operation can be seen in the East Family Brethren's Shop and the products of that operation can be purchased in the Pleasant Hill craft shop.

**LEFT** A Pleasant Hill blacksmith works at a forge in a shop near the West Family House. Note the racks of horseshoes in the front left and right rear. (circa 1910)

(PHOTO BY JOHN BUCKLEY)

**LEFT** A group of Sisters are walking from the Centre Family Dwelling to the Meeting House across the turnpike. This turnpike bisected the Pleasant Hill community and connected the cities of Lexington and Harrodsburg. (circa 1890)

**ABOVE** This group of Brethren and young Sisters pose's outside a stone farm building. In the era before American society had made many institutional arrangements for the care of orphans, the Shakers gladly accepted these children into their communities.

**RIGHT** This former Pleasant Hill warehouse on the Kentucky River was converted to the sawmill you see here. The addition on the right was built in 1864. The Shakers are often credited with the invention of the circular saw, and—although the story of the tool's Shaker creation may be apocryphal—there is no doubt that Shaker sawyers at Pleasant Hill and elsewhere embraced this revolutionary tool. In 1868, the Pleasant Hill community purchased a 12hp steam engine to power a large circular saw.

# The Pleasant Hill
# Woodshop Today

The Interpreter's Manual given to employees working in the woodshop (and elsewhere in the village) explains that "Pleasant Hill is devoted to the correct, informative interpretation of the Shakers and their time at Pleasant Hill. The principal means of achieving that goal is through the excellent presentation of costumed interpreters." Toward that end, one room in the East Family Workshop has been set up to act as a functioning woodshop with one side partitioned off to allow visitors to enter the shop and watch as the craftsmen work.

The shop produces oval boxes, hangers, broom handles, clothes pins, buckets and other types of Shaker woodenware which are then sold in the craft shop. The craftsmen working in that shop also answer visitor's questions about the practice of the crafts they demonstrate.

Bob Roemisch, one of the craftsmen currently working there, came to Pleasant Hill with a woodworking background. At the time of my visit in March of 2006, Roemisch had been working in the shop for eight months. Mark Ross, another of the craftsmen working there, had been in the position for five years at the time of my visit. His background is in social and computer work.

During the winter months, when there are fewer visitors, the craftsmen spend much of their time making woodenware. In the peak tourist months, they often spend entire days talking to visitors.

**ABOVE** Bob Roemisch levels a surface on a turning blank using an antique trying plane, not of Pleasant Hill origin.

(PHOTO: KERRY PIERCE)

**LEFT** Mark Ross turns a whisk broom handle on a period reproduction lathe, of a type likely similar to those used by 19th-century Shaker craftsmen.

"*Most pieces (of Western Shaker work) are very well constructed, convey a feeling of strength, and ...are honest expressions of cabinetmakers working in a style they knew best.*"

JOHN KASSAY IN *THE BOOK OF SHAKER FURNITURE*

*"Members of the church of God...are forbidden to make anything for Believers that will have a tendency to feed...pride and vanity."*

"Millennial Laws" 1845

# Design Features of Pleasant Hill Furniture

Although Ann Lee, the Prophetess who led the very first group of Shakers into the American wilderness of New York State, did not herself write, her views on all things Shaker eventually became codified in the "Millennial Laws" the most comprehensive edition of which was published in 1845, years after her death. Although most of the material in those laws refers to issues of worship and personal conduct, some of it touches on the subject of furnishings for Shaker dwellings and can provide modern students of Shaker design some insight into Ann Lee's thinking. The following line from the "Millennial Laws", for example, provides a theoretical foundation for the design of furniture and architecture: "Beadings, mouldings, and cornices which are merely for fancy may not be made by Believers."

Over the next century, this and other similar direc-

tives guided the hands of Shaker craftsmen as they designed and constructed the buildings and furnishings for their living environments. In addition, when the Shakers purchased goods from the World, as was the case, for example, with many of the timepieces so necessary in the regimented lifestyle of these communalists, they stripped away superfluous ornamentation before adopting those items into their culture.

But Shaker furniture didn't spring fully formed from the directives of Ann Lee. That furniture was firmly rooted in the country furniture of the period in which it was built. The first Pleasant Hill makers—Kentuckians who migrated to the region from eastern states—brought with them the design vocabularies of country furniture in those eastern states. Later, as Kentucky craftsmen in the World began to develop an identifiable regional style, that style, too, was added to the Pleasant Hill mix. What resulted was an aesthetic that is in most cases both identifiably Shaker and identifiably Western. (Western in this context refers to communities in the Western extremity of the Shaker nation, like the Pleasant Hill and South Union communities in Kentucky.)

*"All work done, or things made in the church for their own use, ought to be faithfully and well done, but plain and without superfluity."*
SHAKER JOSEPH MEACHAM, 1790

This gravel road was once the turnpike, and later US 68, which connected Pleasant Hill to the outside world. In the 1960s US 68 was rerouted to run along the southern edge of the Pleasant Hill property. This move made it possible to begin the restoration of Pleasant Hill.

When the Shakers stripped surface ornamentation from period furniture, they drew our attention to the forms underlying that ornamentation.

Instead of carving and veneering, we see the height and width of chests and cupboards. We see the height and width of drawers and doors. We see pattern as drawers ascend a chest front, as doors move across a cupboard

In some cases, these basic forms are arranged according to furniture-making tradition, when, for example, a set of drawers is graduated from a largest bottom drawer to a smallest top drawer. The cupboard over drawers (photo at top left) exhibits this type of graduation. The bottom drawer front is $8\frac{7}{8}$" high, the next one up measures $8\frac{1}{8}$", the next one up measures 7" and the top drawer measures only $5\frac{7}{8}$". This orderly progression, from widest at the bottom to least wide at the top, is one our experience with drawers encourages us to accept.

At other times, however, Shaker craftsmen manipulated these basic forms for reasons of function of which we may now be unaware. The drawers of the cupboard over chest (photo bottom left) were graduated in a way that is less familiar, a way that was perhaps intended to suit a particular use. Instead of the largest drawer being at the bottom, the drawers of this cupboard over chest are graduated in reverse, with the largest drawer at the top. The bottom drawer front measures 8" high, the next one up measures $9\frac{1}{2}$", and the top drawer measures 10".

Why?

It seems unlikely that the maker learned his craft this way. There is a centuries-old tradition of graduating drawers the way they are graduated in the chest of drawers in the top photo. More likely, the maker was meeting a particular need in the Shaker community, one that required a large drawer at waist height.

My first experience with this kind of design eccentricity made me a little uncomfortable. Thirty years ago, when I discovered Shaker furniture, I had little experience with work that didn't follow the familiar patterns of classical American period furniture. Shaker focus on simplicity and function opened my eyes, demonstrating to me that there are other "right" ways to design a piece of furniture, and these ways were not confined to matters of drawer graduation.

In the World, table, chest and cupboard tops of the period were usually made with shaped edges. At the very least, these edges were given a slight radius, but many Pleasant Hill tops were simply cut square. The top of the chest of drawers (top opposite page) is one example. The intermediate top in the cupboard over chest (the top of the drawer unit) is another.

Here, too, we are forced to see, not the embellishment of the basic form—a molded edge—but the form itself, the simple, unsoftened rectangle of wood that

**TOP** This stately cupboard on chest, poised on its dainty tiptoes, presents a style of drawer graduation we have come to regard as normal, having its largest drawer at the bottom and its smallest drawer at the top.

**BOTTOM** The drawers of this cupboard over chest are graduated in what we might see as reverse order with the smallest drawer at the bottom and the largest drawer at the top.

makes up the chest top.

Shaker furniture, with its unadorned squares, rectangles and cylinders, forces us to look with fresh eyes at the fundamental shapes which, combined, make up a piece of furniture. In Shaker hands, these shapes were not simply blank canvasses on which the craftsman could seduce the eye with carving, veneering and molding. They are shapes worthy of our appreciation in their own right. There is beauty in a simple rectangle, in a simple square, in a simple circle. Shakers Calvin Green and Seth Youngs Wells explained it this way in *A Summary View of the Millennial Church or United Society of Believers* published in 1823: "Any thing may, with strict propriety, be called perfect, which perfectly answers the purpose for which it was designed. A circle may be called a perfect circle when it is perfectly round…." It is the pursuit of this state of fundamental perfection, coupled with the primacy of function, that distinguishes the very best Shaker furniture.

There are, of course, some details of Pleasant Hill furniture in which craftsmen deviated from this focus on basic forms. Many of the early chests of drawers have turned feet which present a succession of coves and beads that seem out of place on a piece that otherwise exhibits little embellishment. Each foot of the chest of drawers (in photo at right) includes a pair of wide coves, each topped by a narrow bead.

In addition, each of the drawer fronts is framed in a scratched narrow bead meant to simulate a decorative effect seen on much high-style furniture of the period. This high-style furniture often featured drawer fronts framed in thin mitered strips tacked in place so that the front edges of these strips, rounded to a bead, were standing just proud of the drawer front. Sometimes these strips, called cock beading, were tacked to the drawer front itself. Sometimes they were tacked to the opening in which the drawer front was housed.

Cock beading provided an appealing detail to high-style furniture, but it represented a significant investment of time, an investment that makers of simpler county furniture could not always justify. As a result, country furniture makers in Kentucky, and elsewhere, often created a simulated cock beading around drawer fronts. In the case of very large drawer fronts, that cock beading might be created with a side-bead plane (a kind of molding plane), but much more often, the craftsman would use a shop-made tool called a scratch stock. A scratch stock is simply a bit of thin metal fixed in a wooden holder. The bit of thin metal would be cut with the shape of a bead and quirk (a narrow recessed part of a molding). It would then be dragged around the perimeter of the drawer front, scratching out a little bead, which, at least at a distance, resembled a cock bead. In

The Pleasant Hill chest of drawers is a study in Shaker simplicity, with the exception of two details: the decorative turnings on the feet, and the scratch-stock simulated cock bead surrounding each drawer front.

the hands of a skilled craftsman, this lowly tool could produce a reasonable facsimile, but more often scratch-stock cock beads were often crudely formed, particularly on the ends of drawers where the scratch stock had to be dragged across the grain.

The photo (page 48) shows a bead scratched onto the drawer fronts of the Pleasant Hill chest of drawer shown above.

Such deviations from the theoretical foundation of Shaker furniture do not, in my view, detract from the beauty of that furniture. The bits of decorative turning and scratched cock bead are nothing more than minor imperfections that serve to put a human signature on the work of the Pleasant Hill craftsmen.

## *"Hands to work and hearts to God"*
### Mother Ann Lee

It's impossible to understand the Shakers without appreciating the importance of work in their culture. Their movement began at a time when the mere maintenance of human life required a significant output of labor. But of course, the Shakers of Pleasant Hill did much more than maintain life. In the first three decades

The scratch-stock cock bead on this chest of drawers retains a crisp appearance even in this close-up.

of the 19th century, they erected a community in the Kentucky wilderness that remains today as a monument to human effort.

Anyone who tours the restored Shaker community at Pleasant Hill will be struck by the amount of labor that community represents. The Centre Family Dwelling shown page 157, built to provide living accommodations for 100 Shakers, is made of hand-cut limestone blocks each one quarried by the Shakers and each one transported to the building site by the Shakers and each one hoisted into place by the Shakers. Then, once the enormous facility had been erected, it was fitted with windows and trim, all made by hand, and filled with furniture, also made by hand.

This single structure (one of many at Pleasant Hill) represents an enormous investment of human labor—labor which the Shakers offered as an act of devotion to God. It is in this context of sanctified labor that the third element of Shaker furniture-making comes into play. It wasn't enough that furniture be simple and functional; it must also present a physical manifestation of the sanctity of work.

Simplicity, function, and sanctity—these are some of the identifying characteristics of the best Shaker furniture, and these are characteristics that can be read in much of the furniture that is attributed to Pleasant Hill makers.

### "Shaker chairs were typically light but sturdy"
JUNE SPRIGG AND DAVID LARKIN IN
SHAKER WORK, LIFE, AND ART

Pleasant Hill furniture makers were aware of the work being produced in the world. Many of these makers were simply converts who came, as adults, into the community, bringing with them intimate knowledge of the world they'd left behind. Plus, throughout its history, the Pleasant Hill community was actively involved in

trading with the world. This pollination of Shaker vision by regional worldly influences gave the furniture of Pleasant Hill a character that is not quite like that of the furniture produced in Eastern Shaker communities.

One of the characteristics that distinguishes high-style furniture from its country cousin is the use of thin material. Builders of high-style furniture recognized a need to match thickness to application, a need to use, for example, half-inch material in situations in which thicker material would look clumsy. Obviously a reduction in thickness doesn't enable a piece to better carry a load. The reduction is necessary to impart a measure of visual grace.

Some Pleasant Hill work acknowledges this aesthetic truth. Like the Shaker furniture of Eastern communities, this work conveys a feeling of lightness through the use of thin material. The hanging cupboard (top opposite page) illustrates this principle. Although it is supported by an unseen hidden top measuring $7/8$" thick, the top we do see is only $3/8$" thick, and a further sense of lightness is conveyed via the radiused edge formed on that $3/8$" top.

According to John T. Kirk, the author of *The Shaker World*, the appearance of lightness and fragility is a notion that, in the case of one New Lebanon drying rack the Shakers pushed "almost to silliness" with posts measuring only $13/16$" square. He further describes the seat rungs of a pair of Canterbury cane-seated chairs as "almost ridiculously insubstantial." This style of construction was possible in a community in which care of the acoutrements of life was mandated by Millennial Law, which, among other things, prohibited leaning chairs back against a wall, in fact, prohibited even putting one's feet on the rungs of a chair for fear of wearing out that rung.

Twenty years ago, when I was building my first Shaker rockers, I made a number of examples out of cherry which I had, at least in my mind, turned to perhaps foolishly frail dimensions, with posts only $1 1/4$" in diameter and rungs no more than $3/4$" in diameter at their centerpoints. Today, when I build those same chairs, I use diameters of $1 3/8$" and $7/8$". But I should also point out that those early "frail" rockers of mine are still in use in homes scattered across Southern Ohio.

Much Pleasant Hill furniture, however, is built to a different standard, making use of thick material in contexts in which many makers in Eastern Shaker communities would have used thin material.

The top of the little table with eight-sided legs (lower opposite page) is one example. The top of that table measures a full $7/8$" thick. A table of similar size (with a top $1/2$" narrower but over 7" longer) from the Hancock community, a table drawn by John Kassay in

*The Book of Shaker Furniture* is fitted with a top only $^7/_{16}$" thick (although it is banded in $^9/_{16}$"-wide strips, presumably to keep notions like buttons from falling to the floor). Even if we include the raised banding as part of the top's thickness, it still measures $^5/_{16}$" less than the top of the Pleasant Hill table.

The extra thickness on the Pleasant Hill table might have resulted from nothing more than workshop fatigue, since the top still has what appear to be the marks of a large circular saw, marks a more energetic craftsman would have planed away. This would have resulted in a top that was both thinner and lighter appearing. The apron sections on this table are also thicker than necessary, measuring between 1" and $1^1/_8$" in thickness, although this thickness isn't visible. And while the legs on this table are thinner than on many other Pleasant Hill tables, they are thicker than the legs of many Eastern tables of similar proportions.

In fact, it is in the legs of Pleasant Hill tables that the West's preference for parts thick in cross section is most apparent. The legs of the Leander Gettys work table (following page) are simply massive, with the square upper sections measuring $3^3/_8$" on a side. Certainly: the table is large, but there are examples of Eastern Shaker tables of similar square footage built with less substantial undercarriages. Also, it's not just the maximum thickness of the parts that gives these legs their visual bulk. It's the fact that the legs retain most of this thickness along most of their lengths. Large tables with heavy legs made in Eastern communities have much of their thickness cut away as the legs descend to the floor, resulting in a leg that appears much lighter.

There is, however, one genre of Pleasant Hill furniture making that sometimes runs counter to this preference for parts thick in cross section. Although the classic Pleasant Hill rocking chair has fairly robust posts—most have the typical Shaker maximum diameter of $1^3/_8$"—some Pleasant Hill side chairs have much more delicate posts. Some, in fact, appear too delicate to support their own weight, let alone the weight of a human body.

It's difficult to account for the presence of these few lightly-constructed side chairs. Since the elements from which they are constructed are exceptions to the nearly universal Pleasant Hill preference for thick parts, it's tempting to view these anomalous chairs as perhaps the work of a single craftsman, perhaps someone imported from an Eastern community. And it's also possible—given the complicated and cloudy provenance of some Pleasant Hill work—that the chairs might have slipped unnoted from an Eastern community into Pleasant Hill.

Pleasant Hill chairs, like the chairs of other Shaker communities, developed distinctive features which are

**TOP** This Pleasant Hill hanging cupboard conveys a feeling of lightness thanks, in part, to the radiussed $^3/_8$" top.

**BOTTOM** The thickness of the top and legs of this Pleasant Hill side table gives it a more muscular look than side tables of similar size made in Eastern communities.

Eastern chairs. The Western vases taper from a midpoint up toward a shoulder just under the arm and down to a shoulder just above the seat rungs.

Several years ago, I reproduced a rocker made in the North Union, Ohio, community with this Western-style vase, and while the Pleasant Hill vases I studied for this book were generally like this North Union vase, the Pleasant Hill vases demonstrated two characteristics not found on the vases of other Western chairs I've studied.

First, the Pleasant Hill vase is typically more elongated than similar vases on other Western chairs. Second, the Pleasant Hill vase typically has three scribed lines marking its midpoint.

### *"From each according to his ability"*
#### FATHER JOSEPH MEACHAN

In the evening of my next-to-the-last day at Pleasant Hill during my summer 2005 visit, I went alone into the rooms above the Meeting House. These were the rooms in which the community's Elders and Eldresses had once lived. They were fitted with a good deal of original Pleasant Hill furniture and probably looked much as they had 150 years ago.

It had been a blistering day, and the rooms were not air-conditioned. Even in the twilight of late evening, the air was hot and close, but spending time alone in these rooms was important to me, so important that I didn't notice the heat until later, after I'd left the Meeting House.

I kept my hands folded behind my back in what I now think was an unconscious attitude of respect for the

identifiably different from equivalent features on chairs from other communities. One of these is the placement of the mushroom caps on armed rockers. Mushroom caps on Eastern chairs are typically centered on the through tenons at the tops of the front posts. These tenons penetrate the arms and then penetrate into the caps a short distance, holding the caps in place. But the mushroom caps on most armed Pleasant Hill rockers are offset, ahead and to the outside of the top of the front post, with the front post penetrating through the arm behind the mushroom cap. The cap on these chairs is then held in place with either screws or wood pegs which attach them to a short extension of the arm. This feature might have been an attempt to put that cap in a position in which the palm of the hand more naturally falls.

One exception to this rule is the mushroom cap on the rocking chair with arms (top right). The maker of that chair followed the Eastern community tradition of placing the mushroom cap at the top of the front post.

Another distinctive feature of Pleasant Hill chairs is the post finial. Like the post finials on chairs in other Shaker communities, the post finials on Pleasant Hill chairs evolved into a distinctive shape, one some Pleasant Hill staffers refer to with the aptly turned phrase an "upside-down bowling pin". This finial rises from a usually fairly abrupt shoulder to a narrow throat which then widens to an elongated bulb that is rounded on top.

Also, the vases on the front posts under the arms of Western chairs demonstrate a form that is identifiably different than the form of the vases on

In the earlier examples of Pleasant Hill casework, legs tended to be more ornate than in examples dating from the mid-century on. The legs on these earlier pieces often exhibit beads and coves. Later pieces, like the Gettys work table in Image #21, are more severe in form, with long, unbroken tapers that extend from the square upper section to the floor. Tim Rieman and Jean Burks, the authors of *The Complete Book of Shaker Furniture*, suggest that this stylistic change might have been a reaction to the fundamentalist revival of the 1840s.

In addition to this severity, these later legs are typified by a heaviness not found in the legs of furniture created in Eastern Shaker communities. This is most evident in the leg of the Gettys work table at right, which is remarkably thick all the way from the squared apron section to the floor. The bed leg at center left is similarly massive from square shoulder to floor.

Another feature of Pleasant Hill legs is the usually abrupt transition from square apron section to round (or octagonal) lower section. The side table leg (left), the bed leg (left, center) and the chest-on-chest leg (lower right, center) all have transitionless sawn shoulders below the square apron section. The Getty's work table leg exhibits a minimal turned transition at the shoulder, and the cupboard-on-chest leg (upper right, center) is the only leg on this page with a fully developed transition from square apron section to turned lower section. Perhaps, not coincidentally, it is also the most delicate leg on this page. (Drawing: Kerry Pierce.)

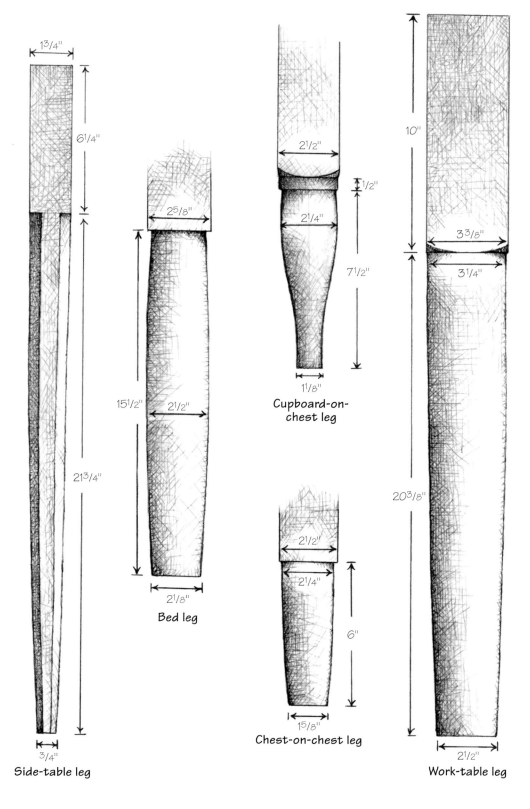

Side-table leg

Bed leg

Cupboard-on-chest leg

Chest-on-chest leg

Work-table leg

Elders and Eldresses who had once lived in these rooms. What they and the men and women in their charge had accomplished here in the Kentucky wilderness in the first half of the 19th century, working largely with hand tools, is almost beyond belief.

I looked at lamps, at a ledger, at a marvelous curly cherry secretary. I looked at oval boxes and blanket chests and simple Shaker beds, at rugs, at a mirror, at all the products of Shaker craft on display there.

Then in the hallway that connected the rooms, I studied each of the over-sized black-and-white photos of 19th-century Pleasant Hill Shakers that hung there, trying to get a sense, via these images, of who these people had been.

The rooms were quiet, the silence broken only by the faint sounds of my feet moving across the wood floors. The only light was the muted late-evening glow coming through the second floor windows.

I like to puzzle over the historical origins of Shaker furniture. I want to know the circumstances that lead to

**TOP LEFT** Pedestal stands like this example were fairly common products of Pleasant Hill workshops. Few, however, carry the history of this particular stand. The ovolo-cornered top was once the lapboard for Sister Mary Carmichael Settles (1836-1923), the last living Pleasant Hill Shaker, who had joined the community as a widow with two children. After Settle's death, her granddaughter had the lapboard placed on this pedestal. The stand then came into the possession of Hazel Hamilton, a dealer in Shaker furniture. Hamilton had the lapboard removed from this base and replaced with a more "Shakeresque" round top. Later, when the stand and lapboard were returned to the Pleasant Hill community, the two original parts were re-united.

Unfortunately, the craftsman who re-united them didn't properly align the base and top. The tops of Shaker tripod stands of this type should be aligned so that that one of the top's long sides is parallel to a line connecting the ends of two of the tripod feet.

**BOTTOM LEFT** The legs on this table exhibit the typically abrupt Pleasant Hill transition from square upper section to turned lower section. The legs are atypical in their relatively thin diameter.

**RIGHT** In addition to focusing our attention on the basic forms of a piece of furniture, the removal of ornamentation has other consequences. One of these, long understood by Shaker craftsmen, is that the simpler the basic form, the better the setting for the display of figured material. This magnificent curly cherry secretary stands in one of the rooms on the second floor of the Meeting House. If the secretary had been decorated with carving or veneering or molding, the effect of the curly cherry might have been compromised.

its creation, but I'm even more interested in the work's emotional origins.

Did the craftsman who made the sponge-painted oval boxes in the quarters above the Meeting House feel the same pride in his workmanship I feel in mine? And what about the maker of that magnificent secretary? Did he step back and admire the beauty and strength of the piece he'd built with his own hands? To have seen it as a product of his efforts would have been antithetical to Shaker belief, but would it have been possible to have succeeded so brilliantly without taking personal satisfaction in the accomplishment?

That is, I think, the essential paradox of Shaker furniture. When it is good, as it is in so many Pleasant Hill pieces, it is very, very good. It is work which, for most modern makers, would be nourishing meals for healthy egos. Is it possible that the 19th-century Pleasant Hill craftsmen who produced this work could have done so without feeling the pride we would have felt in their places?

# The Construction of Casework in the Pleasant Hill Collection

I've been working in the Shaker genre for over twenty-five years, and for much of that time, I've been writing about the stuff I build in an effort to share with others what I have learned about Shaker design principles and construction methods. Like most contemporary makers of Shaker work, I have found the drawing books of Ejner Handberg (Berkshire Traveler Press) to be rich sources of ideas—although there is little in Handberg's books about how the pieces he measured were assembled.

That kind of technical information can best be found in John Kassay's magnificent volume: *The Book of Shaker Furniture* (University of Massachusetts Press), a book I've encountered on the bench of just about every maker of Shaker furniture I've ever visited. But even in the cases of those pieces so beautifully drawn by Kassay, there are bits and pieces of missing and/or puzzling information that force makers like myself to offer up our best guesses.

For example, in my book *Authentic Shaker Fur-*

niture (Popular Woodworking Books 2004), I documented the recreation of a Shaker sewing desk drawn by Kassay. Some of the construction methods detailed in Kassay seemed a little eccentric, suggesting to me that the Shaker craftsman who built the original had added complexities for reasons that are not now known. As a result, I simplified the construction of the desk to eliminate several enigmatically placed pieces of material. I also changed the drawer graduation to an arrangement I found more appealing and I opted to open each drawer with a pair of relatively small knobs, rather than the single oversized knob affixed to each drawer in the original. These are all changes that, in my opinion, constitute improvements on the original, while remaining faithful to the Shaker aesthetic of minimalism and elegance.

In addition, despite the wealth of detail in Kassay's many drawings of the piece, there are no references in those drawings to the methods used by the Shaker builder to fasten in place the desk's two different tops. So here, too, I had to proceed guided by my instincts and experience. The result is a piece that, although recognizably Shaker, is not an exact replica of any Shaker original.

And this circumstance is not at all unusual.

Although I've built and sold hundreds of pieces of "Shaker" work, I can't recall a single one of those pieces that was an absolute replica of any specific Shaker original. All were modified to a greater or lesser extent to suit my tastes and/or those of my clients. Sometimes the changes were nothing more than the substitution of one material for another. At other times, the changes were more comprehensive, as in the case of the Shaker sewing desk that appeared in *Authentic Shaker Furniture*.

I think this approach is common among contemporary makers of Shaker-inspired work. We rarely produce exact replicas of specific Shaker originals. Instead, we do what the 19th-century Shaker craftsmen themselves did, we take a form that has been passed down to us from earlier makers and re-create that form in the light of our own tastes and experiences.

### Built the Way Furniture Should Be Built

Most of the furniture in the Pleasant Hill collection is well conceived and well executed, some of it brilliantly so. The cupboard over chest of drawers (see upper photo on page 56), signed and dated by Charles Hamlin in 1877, is one such piece. This towering monument to the art of

**TOP** This signed piece by Charles Hamlin bears the date "Jan 30th 1877", although some authorities believe it is an earlier construction.

**BOTTOM** These probably hand-made escutcheons integrate nicely into the expansive wood doors of the Hamlin cupboard over chest of drawers.

furniture making has a weight and presence rivaling that of large, high-style casework built in the World.

A trio of enormous frame-and-panel doors conceal the cupboard's interior. The geometry of these doors consists of two horizontal series of rectangles unadorned by shaped edges. Above the doors, the case is surmounted by a wide cove molding anchored in place by a pair of horizontal fillets. In the World, the doors would have been framed in molded edges and the crown molding would have presented a clutter of shadow lines. Such an iteration would certainly have had appeal,

but for someone with my preference for simplicity, the straightforward handling of forms in the Hamlin piece has even more appeal.

For me, this piece comes most sharply into focus when I examine the tiny, probably shop-made, escutcheons on the doors (lower photo this page). The maker wisely chose to avoid the visual distraction of metal escutcheons on the front of a piece that, except for the slivers of visible hinge pins, is an unbroken seascape of wood.

Good joinery is evident throughout the piece. The lower case is built between a pair of post-and-panel ends with mortise-and-tenon joinery used to frame the drawers, which are nicely dovetailed themselves. The frame-and-panel doors of the upper case also employ mortise-and-tenon joinery, and the crown molding is held in place with a series of glue blocks.

This use of good wood-to-wood joinery is evident almost everywhere in the Pleasant Hill collection. There are, however, some exceptions; and that's where I think the story of Pleasant Hill joinery becomes very intriguing.

### The Lowly Nail

Shaker furniture makers have been revered, in particular since the Shaker chairmaking operation of New Lebanon under the direction of Brother Robert Wagan won acclaim at the Philadelphia Centennial Exhibition in 1876. In fact at one point in the mid-20th century, this reverence had reached such a point that any country piece assembled with dovetails was apt to be identified as Shaker. That perception was not only inaccurate (as you'll see, there is some Shaker furniture built to different standards of craftsmanship than you might expect); that perception was also unfair to those craftsmen in the World who made carefully constructed country furniture using dovetails, as well as many other signatures of fine workmanship.

While the craftsmanship in the very best Shaker work did, in fact, rival high-style furniture of the period, the Shakers were capable of employing techniques, even in this best work, that modern craftsmen might find disconcerting.

For example, Shaker craftsmen made widespread use of nails— and not just for the installation of moldings, but also for structural applications.

The miniature blanket chest (upper photo page 57) illustrates this point. The case and plinth are, of course, nicely dovetailed, but the bottom of the chest is held in place through the use of nails driven through the chest front and back into the edges of the chest bottom. This is not what most contemporary makers would describe as good joinery. In fact, because the chest bottom has shrunk across its width, there are unsightly gaps visible on each side of that bottom panel when you look down into the open chest from above.

More properly that bottom should have been fitted into grooves plowed on the insides of the chest sides and ends. That technique would have eliminated not only the nails that hold the bottom in place, but also the unsightly gaps, by allowing the builder to conceal extra width on the bottom panel in the grooves on either side. The bottom could then have shrunk in width without creating visible gaps on either side.

The hanging cupboard (lower photo this page), although an elegant manifestation of the Shaker aesthetic, uses nails for nearly all its structural elements. The sides, top and bottom are nailed together. The bottom and back are nailed in place, as is the frame around the door. Only the door itself exhibits the kind of joinery, through tenons, that could be identified as truly appropriate for that application.

But, having said that, I must then remind myself that the cabinet is still intact, 150 years after its construction. Yes, I would have preferred to find in the cabinet the kind of joinery that a first-class modern maker would employ in assembling such a piece. Specifically, I would have preferred that the cabinet's sides, top and bottom be assembled with dovetails, and I would have preferred to find mortise-and-tenon joinery in the frame around the door, but my preferences have more to do with my woodworking prejudices than with the ability of the piece to survive from one generation to the next.

And I have first-hand knowledge that my joinery prejudices aren't necessarily supported by the facts. In the small woods beside my shop, we have a chicken coop that has a door I made almost 20 years ago from some common-grade cherry boards which, because of knots and wane and sap streaks, were just not good enough to be used in furniture. I built the door when the cherry was green and soft enough to be nailed easily. In the twenty years since its construction, the cherry has hardened and shrunk down around those nails, clenching each in a death grip. That door will now never come apart.

I know hardwood furniture nailed together in such a way is all but indestructible, but my woodworking prejudices, honed by thirty years of cutting wood-to-wood joinery, are difficult to ignore.

**ABOVE RIGHT** This nicely proportioned miniature blanket chest features dovetailed joinery on the case itself and simple nails to hold in place the chest's bottom.

**BOTTOM RIGHT** Many Shaker utilitarian pieces, like this hanging cupboard, made use of nails in structural contexts.

## The Intersection of Joinery and Aesthetics

The hanging cupboard is made of poplar, a soft material usually green in color, often exhibiting wide areas of gray and black. Poplar is an easily worked species, frequently used by midwestern cabinetmakers as a secondary wood for drawer sides and bottoms, as well as the interior structural components of cabinets featuring more desirable primary woods, like cherry or walnut. Poplar is not, however, often itself used as a primary wood, except in the case of utilitarian furniture, like this hanging cupboard.

**ABOVE** Shaker craftsmen used nails as structural devices even when those nails were visible and as a result became a part of a piece's aesthetic. This chest of drawers, for example, has nails driven through the tenons of its mortise-and-tenon front, as well as nails driven down through the top into the posts on the ends of the chest.

**LEFT** This detail shows the head of a nail driven through a mortise-and-tenon joint.

I am, therefore, more inclined to accept nailed construction in such a piece. Plus, the cupboard was given a heavy red stain which, when it was new, probably all but obliterated any sign of the nails in the finished piece.

The Pleasant Hill craftsmen, however, didn't restrict the use of nails to utilitarian furniture made of poplar and stained red. They also made widespread use of nails in the construction of furniture made of the finest locally available materials, in the construction of pieces finished natural, using these nails even in places where they could be easily seen.

The chest of drawers (upper photo below) is one such piece. The chest has its mortise-and-tenoned frame pegged together, not with wood pegs, but with nails, the heads of which are clearly visible.

For many years, I repaired antique furniture in my shop, and I sometimes came across constructions like the one appearing in the lower detail photo. Usually, however, the nail driven through the tenon was a fairly recent addition. Someone, perhaps the current owner, perhaps another recent owner, had opted to fix a weakened glue joint by driving a nail through a tenon. But I suspect the nails in this Pleasant Hill chest of drawers were driven through the tenons by the Shaker craftsman who built the piece.

I say this for several reasons. First, there is the evident age of the nails. They have been in place so long that the iron in the nails has leached into the surrounding wood, darkening its color. Second, this piece, and others like it in the Pleasant Hill collection, made such widespread use of nails in similar contexts that this form of joinery appears to have been an accepted method of assembly in the Pleasant Hill workshops. And third, this is a technique I have often seen not only in the work of this Shaker community. but also in the work of other Shaker communities (as well as in the work of many country furniture makers of the period in the World).

In the Pleasant Hill furniture I examined, nails showed up in other contexts as well. Although cabinet tops were typically fastened in place with pocket screws (upper photo page 59), this method of attachment seems to have been routinely reinforced by nails driven down through the top into the end grain of a table or chest's posts (lower photo page 59). I have to admit this particular application puzzles me because nails driven into end grain have little holding power, but it may be that when driven into relatively green end grain, the holding power becomes better as the material shrinks around the shank of the nail.

When they're used to peg tenons or to hold down a top, this use of nails is not just a matter of joinery; it also becomes a part of the Pleasant Hill aesthetic. These metallic fasteners are visible to the casual viewer, sometimes glinting reflected light into the eye, drawing our attention to something our modern perceptions of joinery tells us should not be there.

It is in this context that the nails used in Pleasant Hill furniture are most problematic for me. I recognize that if you drive a nail through a mortise-and-tenon joint you have created a powerful joint, particularly after the wood has shrunk down around that nail, but I am, nevertheless, troubled by the fact that the nail head is visible in the finished piece.

## The Mystery of the Half-blind Dovetail

When you're cutting dovetails by hand (the only way I know how to cut them and the method used by 19th-century Shakers), the easiest type to cut are through dovetails. Half-blind dovetails are much more time-consuming to create because every socket for every tail must be chopped out with chisels. This doubles the time and effort required to cut a set of dovetails, but there are many applications for which this extra effort is justified.

For example, while through dovetails are perfectly acceptable at the back of a drawer, half-blind dovetails are preferred for attaching the drawer front because half-blind dovetails don't allow the joinery to disturb the look of that drawer front. This is because the ends of

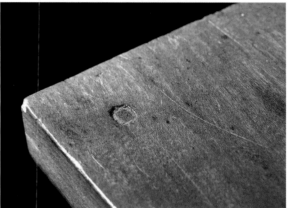

**TOP** Pocket screws, like these crudely formed examples, were often used by Shaker craftsmen to hold tops in place.

**BOTTOM** This nail is driven through the top of the chest of drawers into the chest's end panel.

the tails will be concealed by a covering of wood when the drawer is closed.

It's customary for modern makers who are assembling a case in which all sides are open to the eye to assemble that case with through dovetails. This is because the extra effort required to cut half-blind dovetails seems misplaced when the dovetails can be seen from one side, if not from both. Nevertheless, there are a number of Pleasant Hill blanket chests on which the maker(s) took the time to cut half-blind dovetails on the front corners of the chest but used through dovetails on the back corners. (Photos page 60.)

Why?

If the craftsman's intention was to hide the joinery, full-blind dovetails would have been the correct choice because the half-blind joinery is still visible to an observer standing at the front of the chest. Plus, the backs of these chests feature through dovetails which are visible from both the back and the sides.

And this approach was not used consistently in the creation of Pleasant Hill chests. The miniature blanket chest mentioned earlier in this story was assembled with through dovetails on all four corners, a method that would be used by most modern makers of such casework.

This large Pleasant Hill blanket chest features a proliferation of finely cut dovetails as well as an ingeniously executed bit of joinery uniting the post and rail in the chest's base.

I'm attracted to this puzzle for two reasons. First, I enjoy the process of trying to determine why a maker, separated from me by a century or more, might have chosen to do a thing in a way that, at least to me, seems counter-intuitive. That is I'm drawn by my nosiness, my unvarnished need to pry. But the puzzle is important in another way as well. If I someday decide to reproduce one of these Pleasant Hill blanket chests, what kind of joinery will I use? The one I found in the original or the one that makes the most sense to me?

### The Exuberant Expression of Craftsmanship

Dovetail joinery is the best option when joining the ends of two boards at an angle of 90 degrees. The joint pro-

vides mechanical resistance to separation in one direction while providing a significant amount of glue surface to resist separation in the other direction.

The number of dovetails a craftsman chooses to distribute along a 90 degree corner is determined by the amount of abuse the piece is expected to experience as well as the look the craftsman wants to achieve. If you'll examine the miniature blanket chest shown on (page 57 upper photo), you'll see a fairly typical distribution of pins and tails for a context like this, that is you'll see a fairly small number of fairly wide tails. This is more than enough joinery to keep these sides together. But if you look at the corners of the full-size blanket chest (upper right photo), you'll see a much different situation. The

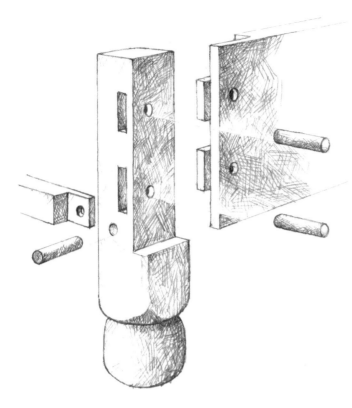

This illustration shows the complicated joinery in the base of the large blanket chest. (Drawing: Kerry Pierce.)

maker of this chest packed that corner with a huge number of pins and tails. This significantly increased the amount of time and effort required to cut and fit the joinery, an increase you probably can't explain simply by taking into account the amount of abuse the chest was likely to receive.

Then why? Why cut all those pins and tails? Why not lighten the work load with a distribution more like that found on the miniature blanket chest.

Before I offer my best guess at an answer, I'd like to draw your attention to one other feature of the full-sized blanket chest. Look at the joinery with which the base is assembled. When I first examined this piece, I didn't really see the many complications presented by this union of post and rail.

But later, after I'd gotten out a pencil and paper and taken the time to articulate the cutting this little flourish of skill would have required, I had what I think is an insight into the mind of the man who made this chest.

He was, I believe, a man who loved joinery, a man who loved the process of carefully fitting one part to another. Maybe that precision was an act of worship or an offering to God. But maybe it was something else as well, something that all of us, regardless of our religious persuasion, can understand. Maybe it was nothing more than an exuberant expression of the sheer joy he found in craftsmanship.

## The Record of What They Knew

I think we study the furniture of our woodworking ancestors for two reasons. First, we want to grow as furniture makers. We want to know what they knew, and the record of what they knew is written in the work that survives them. But there is another motivation that is, to me, even more important. To the extent that it possible when separated from them by a 150-year chasm of time, I want to know what it felt like to be one of the 19th-century Shakers who produced the marvelous furniture now on display at Pleasant Hill. I want to climb inside their woodworking skin, to feel the heft of their tools in my hands, to experience vicariously the joy they found in the simple act of creating beautiful objects in wood.

# The Pleasant Hill
# Collection

### The Furniture Diaspora

In 1910, the twelve remaining Pleasant Hill Shakers signed an agreement with local landowner George Bohon that deeded him the 1500 acres of Shaker land that had not been previously sold to pay off debts incurred by the declining society. In return, Bohon agreed to provide support for those twelve aged Shakers in the final years of their lives. When the last of these twelve, Sister Mary Settles, died in 1923, the Pleasant Hill Shakers were no more, and the 120-year-long experiment in communal living undertaken at Pleasant Hill came to a final, irrevocable end.

In the following decades, the properties once comprising the Pleasant Hill community were put to many uses. Much of the land, of course, was farmed. The buildings hosted several different groups and individuals, some being used as homes for tobacco sharecroppers, another as a tearoom, another as a store and yet another as a filling station. Plus, for many years, right up until the time the Shakertown Corporation began the current restoration of Pleasant Hill in the early 1960s, the Meeting House was used as a Baptist church.

During those early decades of the 20th century, no one made any organized effort to preserve the furniture left behind by the Pleasant Hill Shakers. Some pieces, no doubt, served the transitory tenants of the various Pleasant Hill buildings, being put to use as tables, chairs and desks. Other pieces were simply stolen.

Not everyone who stole from Pleasant Hill benefited from their thievery. Several years ago, an eight-foot-long antique (non-Shaker) bench once used in the visitors center showed up on the doorstep of the Pleasant Hill administrative offices. A note was attached explaining that this piece had been stolen from Pleasant Hill in the early 1970s and had caused years of bad luck for the family that had taken it. The author of the note hoped that returning the bench would lift the curse.

### What Is and What Is Not Pleasant Hill Work

Because of the convoluted provenance of much of the furniture now in the Pleasant Hill collection, it would be difficult to say with absolute certainty that all the pieces in this book are of Pleasant Hill origin.

Several signed pieces of Pleasant Hill work do exist, and one of those is included in this book: the kitchen work table signed L. Gettys. Presumably this indicates Leander Gettys who lived and worked (as a carpenter for at least part of his life according to the 1860 census) at Pleasant Hill from 1844 until he "ingloriously fled" in 1865, according to Pleasant Hill records. In addition, there are several pieces of Pleasant Hill work identified in documents in the Pleasant Hill collection. One such piece is the miniature blanket chest in this book which is identified in a letter saying that Mary Settles, the very last of the Pleasant Hill Shakers, had given the chest to an unnamed man.

But most of the work now in the Pleasant Hill collection lacks this kind of documentary provenance. Some pieces were provisionally identified as Pleasant Hill simply because they were in the buildings of the community when those buildings were purchased prior to restoration. While this is suggestive of a Pleasant Hill origin, it is not conclusive. Some of the work we now identify as Pleasant Hill is stylistically indistinguishable from Kentucky country work of the same period, and it's possible that a post-1910 tenant could have brought into the Pleasant Hill community Kentucky furniture from the world, leaving it at Pleasant Hill on their departure

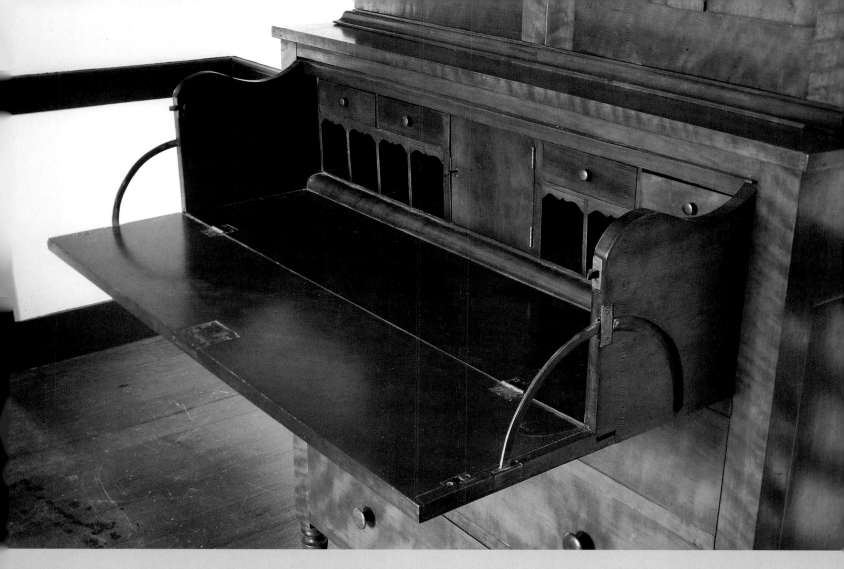

to confound later students of the furniture. Plus, according to the Museum Director Larrie Curry, the Pleasant Hill "Shakers were buying bureaus from the outside world in the 1840s and 50s at the same time they were making them."

Further muddying the waters were the well intentioned efforts of Burwell Marshall. Shortly before World War II, Marshall, a lawyer from Louisville, acquired the heart of the Pleasant Hill community, including the Centre Family and East Family Dwellings. It was his intention to set up a Shaker Museum in the Centre Family Dwelling. Toward that end, he began traveling to the Eastern Shaker communities on buying trips at about, fortuitously, the same time some of those communities were being closed and their portable goods sold off. His purchases were shipped back to Pleasant Hill to become part of the collection in the museum he planned. But his museum never opened, and twenty years later, after selling his Pleasant Hill property to the Shakertown Corporation, Marshall donated to that corporation his east coast acquisitions as well as the Pleasant Hill material he had acquired when he purchased the Pleasant Hill properties.

Unfortunately, this influx of Eastern material wasn't adequately catalogued, and there are pieces now identified as having been a part of the "Marshall Collection" without specifying whether those pieces were original to Pleasant Hill or whether they had been imported by Marshall from one of the Eastern communities.

As I compiled my list of furniture for this book, the lack of clear Pleasant Hill provenance for some of the pieces I considered was both a source of frustration and a source of fascination. It was frustrating to be told that my list of potential objects included pieces likely of Eastern origin, but that fact also added an extra layer of meaning to each of the pieces eliminated in this way. A piece made in New Lebanon, New York, and then shipped to Pleasant Hill, Kentucky, a hundred years later has a layer of history it wouldn't have had if that piece had simply remained in New Lebanon.

The final list of objects for this book, the one represented on the pages that follow, was given passing marks by the person who knows those objects best: Larrie Curry. She reviewed my list and agreed there is no known reason to disqualify any as the product of Pleasant Hill woodshops. In fact, it is her opinion that the available evidence suggests that each piece in the pages that follow is, in fact, of Pleasant Hill origin.

# Rocking Chair with Arms

MATERIAL: *maple*
LOCATION: *first floor Centre Family Dwelling*

My brother Kevin and I spent four days at Pleasant Hill in March of 2006 doing research for this book. While he took measurements and photographed details of the pieces I'd selected, I researched those pieces and their history in the materials the Pleasant Hill Museum Director, Larrie Curry, made available.

Late on my last day at Pleasant Hill, I entered the Centre Family Dwelling for a final look around before I went back to my room to continue reading some of the materials Larrie Curry had given me. Kevin, I knew, was up in a third floor room recording information about three of the pieces I'd chosen in that room, one of which was a very handsome armed rocker.

I wandered up and down the commodious first-floor hall, checking what I saw in each room against a list

I held in my hand. For the past twenty-four hours, that list had remained unchanged, without any additions or deletions. I thought we had attained a nice mix of large and small pieces, of chairs and casework, of furniture and woodenware. And Larrie Curry had gone over the current incarnation of the list just five or six hours earlier and had agreed everything was, to the best of her knowledge, of Pleasant Hill origin.

Then I saw this chair.

I stepped through the gate in the railing intended to keep visitors at a distance.

I think I could remember considering this chair for my list, but there were so many chairs in so many Pleasant Hill buildings that it was hard to be sure. The finial and vase turnings were crisp and clean without the flattened

**LEFT** The quality of this finial is a result of two things. First there is a significant difference between its greatest and least diameters. Second, the radius at the bottom of the finial is a graceful extension of the finial's shape.

**FACING PAGE** This armed rocker is one of the finest in the Pleasant Hill collection. It is typical of other Pleasant Hill rockers in that it is surmounted with the characteristic Pleasant Hill upside-down-bowling-pin finials. Plus it has the recognizably Pleasant Hill vases under the arms, vases which from the midpoint are tapered up toward their tops and down toward their bottoms. It is atypical in that the front posts extend up through the arms into the mushroom caps.

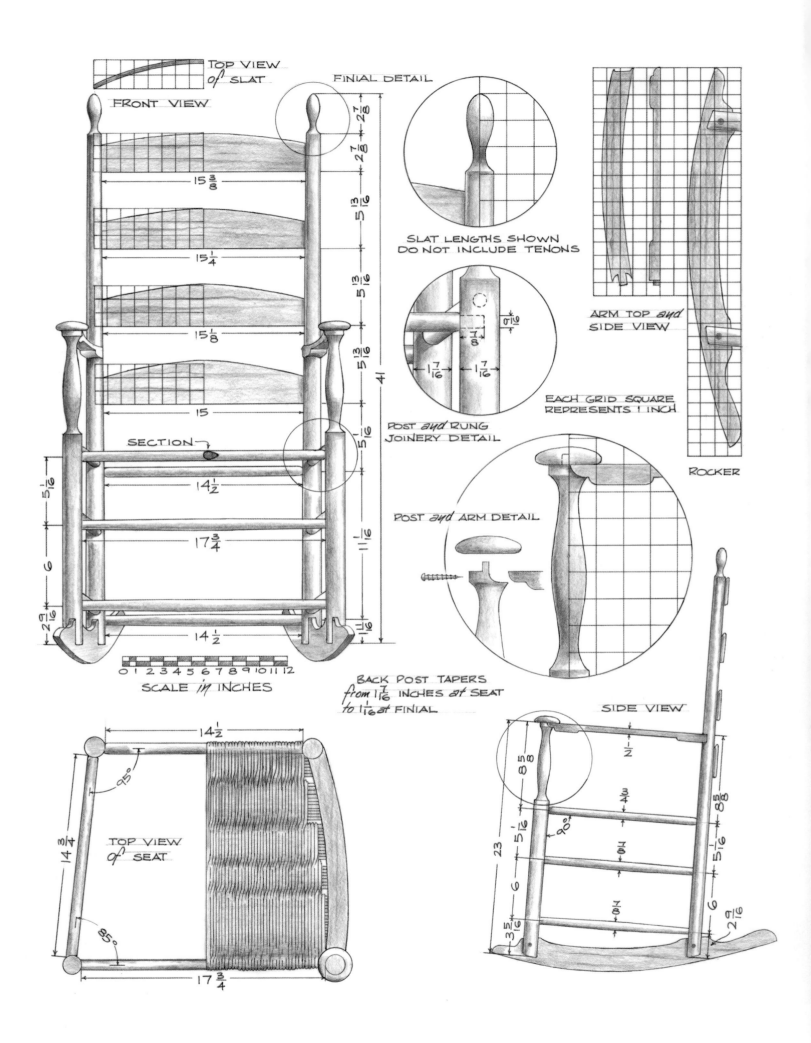

TOP VIEW *of* SLAT

FRONT VIEW

FINIAL DETAIL

SLAT LENGTHS SHOWN
DO NOT INCLUDE TENONS

POST *and* RUNG
JOINERY DETAIL

ARM TOP *and*
SIDE VIEW

EACH GRID SQUARE
REPRESENTS 1 INCH

ROCKER

POST *and* ARM DETAIL

SECTION

SCALE *in* INCHES

0 1 2 3 4 5 6 7 8 9 10 11 12

BACK POST TAPERS
*from* 1 7/16 INCHES *at* SEAT
*to* 1 1/16 *at* FINIAL

TOP VIEW
*of* SEAT

SIDE VIEW

15 3/8

15 1/4

15 1/8

15

14 1/2

17 3/4

14 1/2

2 7/8

2 7/8

5 13/16

5 13/16

5 13/16

5 16

11 16

11 16

41

5 16

6

2 9/16

95°

85°

14 3/4

14 1/2

17 3/4

8 5/8

8 5/8

8 5/8

5 16

5 16

90°

1/2

3/4

4 1/2

7/8

23

6

3 5/16

6

2 9/16

1 7/8

1 7/16

1 7/16

9/16

This Pleasant Hill chair has a lightness and grace that rivals any rocker produced in any of the Eastern Shaker communities.

**LEFT** This is the arm configuration most often seen on Pleasant Hill rockers. The front post penetrates the arm to the rear of the mushroom cap, with the mushroom cap then held in place with a screw.

Compare the shape of this mushroom cap to the one on the opposite page. The radius at the edge of this cap is abrupt. By contrast, the radius on the mushroom cap on the opposite page extends all the way to the center of the cap. This results in a long and visually pleasing line.

Also compare the vase turnings under the arm of this chair to the vase turnings under the arm on the opposite page. Both vases exhibit the same general shape, but the vase on the on the opposite page chair is much more fully realized than is the vase in this photo. In this photo, the tapers above and below the center are simple straight lines, while the tapers on the vase on the opposite page never settle into straightness. Instead the lines present a gradual, and pleasing, ogee curve. Also the radius at the top and bottom of the vase in this chair are quite abrupt, whereas the radii at the top and bottom of the vase on the opposite page chair are continuations of the gentle ogee curve which defines the vase's shape.

**RIGHT** The outside diameter of the vase below the arm rises in a smooth continuous line from the post proper to the arm. The mushroom cap is not simply a disk of wood with a radius cut into its upper edge. Instead, the craftsman created a line that runs all the way from the bottom of the cap to the cap's highest point, at its center.

arcs that could suggest an unsure or lazy craftsman.

I crouched down beside the chair and ran my fingers over the top and bottom surface of the arm. The bottoms of the arms had been relieved in the middle 70-80% of their lengths, then left thicker at the ends where the thickness was needed for joinery. This is a telling detail. There is no structural advantage to this removal of thickness. It's an action taken for purely aesthetic reasons, one that serves to lighten the chair both physically and visually and one that serves to add an appealing detail to an otherwise plain construction.

I sighted down the back ladder. Nicely bent slats. Sometimes the slats reveal unequal bending, with one or two being much more sharply bent than the others. An entire back ladder might slouch one way or the other as

a response to a century or more of age, but when a single slat is out of whack, that fact usually points to carelessness at construction.

This chair was obviously the work of a highly competent craftsman, something not always true of Shaker furniture. This is, in part, a result of the approach that Shaker tradition required craftsmen to take to their work. While a cabinetmaker of the period working in the World would likely have been a cabinetmaker throughout his working life, this was not so in the communal existence of the Shakers. A Shaker who was a chairmaker in February might become a farmer in April and a stone mason in August. Life in a communal society meant that Shaker workmen applied themselves to whatever task was at hand. So the most talented furniture makers sometimes spent parts of their year working at something other than furniture making. And a craftsman who might be best at, say, stone work would be pressed into service in the woodshop.

Freegift Wells, perhaps the best known Shaker chairmaker (after, of course, Robert Wagan), was also a toolmaker, a teacher and an administrator, as well as a manufacturer of many different kinds of wooden objects: broom handles, dipper handles, bowls and curtain rods, plus, much like many of today's amateur craftsmen, Freegift made countless wood handles for fancy writing pens which he sold to the World.

Despite his talent for chairmaking, despite his prodigious output in that craft, Wells obligations to the communal society in which he lived required him to frequently put his hands to work outside the woodshop.

I stepped back and looked at the chair from the side. The widths of the rockers were also relieved in their middle sections in a way that echoed the relief in arm thickness, giving the side profile an appealing aesthetic coherence.

I picked up the chair and carried it up two flights of stairs to the third floor where I startled Kevin, who was lost in his drawing. I explained what I wanted to try,

**LEFT** This finial is pleasing, but when it is placed next to the finial in the photo on page 63, we see it is not as pleasing as it might be. That's largely because the bulb at the top of this finial has a lesser greatest diameter than does the bulb on the finial in the photo on page 65 which results in a slightly less dramatic line as it moves down from the crown of the finial to its base.

**RIGHT** This handsome armed rocker is the piece I almost selected to represent this form. It was only when compared to the more pleasing rocker on page 62 that I removed this fine chair from my list.

smoothly modulated radius which transitioned gracefully to the lower post. By contrast, on the third-floor chair, the vases ended with an abrupt, perfunctory arc.

The mushroom caps were also quite different. The caps on the third-floor chair exhibited flat tops and sharp uniform radii around their circumferences, so uniform they looked router made. The caps on the first floor chair, however, exhibited radii that started fairly steeply at the bottom and then became more and more gradual as they neared the center points on the tops of the caps. This attenuated radius created a much more appealing line.

In the case of the third-floor chair, each of these turned details was executed in a way that suggested that the craftsman at the lathe was simply following a pattern, while those same details on the first-floor rocker were executed by someone who knew how to extract maximum meaning from these simple shapes. One craftsman had been going through the motions, while the other had been intensely "there" in the moment.

Joinery note: There is a large screw that passes through each front post, presumably into the end grain of the arms. This is probably original construction since it appears on other Pleasant Hill chairs, but the installation of the screw is a little crudely done, not up to the standards of the rest of the chair. So I wonder. Plus, despite the widespread presence of steel fasteners in other Shaker (and non-Shaker) chairs, I believe they are simply not a good idea on any construction that must flex in use the way a chair must flex in use. That's because metal screws don't flex. Instead of flexing, they split the surrounding wood. When I reproduce this chair, I'm going to fasten the arm to the front post with a tenon and forget the screw.

Also, the specific details of this joinery are impossible to discern without disassembling the chair, so the resolution the drawings present is our best guess.

picked up the armed rocker in that third-floor bedroom and carried it out to the hall where I placed it beside the one from the first floor. The light was a little dim so I brought out one of the floodlights Kevin was using.

There were both armed Pleasant Hill rockers, and either would fill that slot in my list of representative pieces. Each chair had the characteristic Pleasant Hill finials sometimes described as upside-down bowling pins. Each chair had similar vase-like shapes turned on the front posts under the arms. Each chair had mushroom caps at the end of each arm. But these features were articulated in very different ways.

The bulbs at the tops of the finials on the first-floor chair (photo page 65) had a greater diameter which gave the tapers below the bulbs a more dramatic sweep than the tapers on the third-floor chair (photo above) could achieve. This is an effect of the difference between least and greatest finial diameters: the greater the difference, the more dramatic the line. The vases under the arms of the first-floor chair carried the eye downward to a

with some scraps of $3/4$" birch plywood and a strip of poplar.

Once the cradle is made, drill an $1/8$" hole through each of the cradle's end pieces. These holes will mark the legs' axes of rotation. On the inside surface of one of the cradle's end pieces (which I'll call the headstock end), draw a square $1^3/4$" on a side centered on the legs' axes of rotation with its bottom line parallel to the bottom of the cradle. Then draw a second square exactly the same size and also centered on the legs' axes of rotation that is rotated 45 degrees from the first square. Finally draw a square on the inside surface of the cradle's tailstock end that is centered on the legs' axes of rotation and parallel to the bottom of the cradle. These squares will allow you to align the leg blanks for the sawing of each leg's eight faces.

Drill an extra hole through the end piece on the headstock end. This hole should be placed so that it is apart from the center hole and still inside each of the two squares you drew on the inside of the headstock end piece. The screw you turn into this extra hole will hold the blank in the proper alignment for each pass over the band saw.

Find the center of each end of each leg blank and mark it with a pencil. Then drill a shallow ($1/2$" deep) $1/8$" in diameter hole in the centers of each leg.

Turn a $1^1/4$" #6 drywall screw through all three of the cradle end piece holes so that the points of each screw can just barely be felt on the inside surfaces of the cradle's end pieces.

Hold a leg blank in place so that its centers are positioned directly in line with the center points you marked on the inside of the cradle's end pieces. Then turn the drywall screws on each end of the cradle into the centers of each end of the leg. With the leg blank positioned so that it aligns with the single square you drew on the inside of the tailstock end of the cradle, turn the extra screw on the headstock end of the cradle into the end grain of the blank. This third screw, the set screw, will hold the blank in the correct rotational alignment for cutting the first of the leg's eight facets.

Next you need to make a flexible pattern for marking the leg's facets. I made mine from $1/4$" birch plywood, but stiff cardboard would work just as well. The pattern should be as long as the full $20^7/8$" length of the leg's lower section and the full $1^3/4$" width of the blank. The taper you mark must retain enough of the leg's thickness so that after you've made the band saw cuts, you can plane away the band saw marks without removing any of the leg's finished thickness. After some experimentation, I settled on a width of $1^1/4$" at the foot of the pattern.

Lay the pattern on the blank so that its straight side aligns with one side of the leg blank and the narrow end of the pattern aligns with the foot of the blank. Then

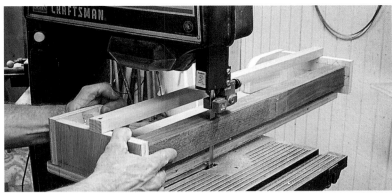

**TOP** Cut the first four tapers by moving the cradle past the band saw blade.

**MIDDLE** After the first four tapers have been cut, fix the untapered apron section of the leg blank in your vise. Then plane away the saw marks on the taper.

**BOTTOM** Leg blank in the cradle after the second set of four facets has been sawn. Notice that the top of the leg blank is aligned with the second of the two squares I drew on the inside of the headstock end piece.

draw a line along the taper.

Place the cradle (with the leg blank attached) on the table of your band saw and cut that first taper. Place the cradle back on the bench, back off the set screw enough so that the leg can be rotated, then rotate the blank 90 degrees (using the pencil squares drawn on the cradle's headstock end piece as your guide), then turn the set screw into this new position, locking the blank in place. Use your pattern to mark this next taper, and return the cradle to the band saw and saw this next facet. Repeat until the first four facets are sawn.

The pattern's flexibility will come into play as you place marks on already sawn (tapered) surfaces.

Then remove the blank from the cradle, plane the four sawn tapers until they're smooth, and reinstall the blank in the cradle via the center screws on each end.

Before you go any further, take a close look at the drawing of the leg and the photo of the finished table. Notice that the facets you've already cut are

**TOP** The tenons can be fine tuned with a shoulder plane or a rabbet plane.

**MIDDLE** Paring chisels will cut the flat in each screw pocket. The rounded excavation can be made with a gouge.

**BOTTOM** This detail of the original table shows how the pocket holes work. Note the clean cuts at the termination of the octagonal shape.

simply tapering extensions of the four sides of the leg's upper, apron section. Notice also the next four facets, those you're about to cut, begin at shoulders which are sawn in a way that connects adjacent faces of the table's square apron section.

If you haven't already done so, with your tri-square and a pencil, mark the bottom of the leg's four-sided apron section. Then mark a location $^3/_8$" in from each end of each of these lines on the leg blank. This will be a total of eight marks, two on each side of the apron section of the leg. Next, with a fine-toothed backsaw, cut the shoulders marking the top of the leg's other four facets. Each saw cut should connect two marks, each $^3/_8$" from the outside edges on two of the leg's adjacent faces. Be sure to cut below the shoulder's finished location so that you'll have material you can pare away in order to produce a finished end grain surface.

The foot of the leg should now be a finished square, measuring something in the area of one inch on a side. If it's a little more or a little less, that's fine. Make a mark $^1/_4$" from the outside of each side of the foot. Here, too, there should be eight marks.

## Working by Eye

The next step is one that may make some woodworkers uncomfortable. Working freehand, draw a line connecting the mark ($^1/_4$" from the outside) at the foot with the mark ($^3/_8$" from the outside) at the bottom of the apron section of the leg. That line will be the line that will form the next facet of the leg. Remember that you're going to further define this line with a plane, so don't worry if it's not absolutely perfect. Close is good enough.

Position the blank so that the top section aligns with the second square you marked on the headstock end of the cradle. (This is the square drawn 45 degrees from the square you made parallel to the base of the cradle.) Turn the set screw into the end grain of the leg blank. Working from the middle of the marked taper, saw toward both ends of the cut.

Repeat this process until the other four sides of the leg's octagonal cross section have been roughed in.

Remove the blank from the cradle and then finish up the tapers with a little plane work guided by your eye.

The objective is to end up with tapers that rise from a foot approximately $^3/_4$" thick, swell outward slightly at the midpoint of the taper, then continue upward to a leg $1^3/_4$" thick, with eight facets approximately $^3/_4$" wide directly below the shoulder.

Holding the blank in your bench vise, use a couple of your favorite planes, and a good paring chisel up under the sawn shoulders, to fine tune the tapers.

If possible, resist the temptation to reach for a measuring tool. This process works best if the only measurements are those made by your unassisted eye. Take a shaving or two from a facet that seems a little thin. (Remember that when you take a shaving, you actually increase the width of the facet.) Then rotate the blank in your vise. Then take another shaving from another facet if you think you need to.

In the fifteen years I've been writing for woodworking magazines, I've had the pleasure of visiting the shops of some of this country's greatest craftsmen, and every single one routinely demonstrated the ability to find the right line, not only by measuring, but also by working with tools that were guided by the unassisted human eye. This isn't a skill they'd had since birth. This was a skill they developed over the course of many years of practice, and it is, I believe, the most important tool in their woodworking arsenal. If a line looks right, it probably is right, even if your rule tells you, you could make it little righter by taking off one more shaving.

Mark and cut the mortises for each of the apron tenons. (This time you should measure.)

## Making the Apron

The apron sections of the Pleasant Hill original were made, I suspect, from bits and pieces of material left over from other jobs. One apron section is 1" thick. Another is $1\frac{1}{8}$" thick, and I think all four sections taper in their thickness. I decided to make mine a consistent 1" thick since that was easiest.

Create the tenon thickness with a couple of passes of each apron section over a stack of dado cutters on your table saw. (I undercut the shoulder on the back side of each tenon about $\frac{1}{16}$" to guarantee a tight shoulder-to-leg fit on the outside of each apron section. I measured that $\frac{1}{16}$" by eye, and I'm sure that if I put a rule on the gap on the back side of each section, some gaps would measure $\frac{1}{16}$" while others might measure $\frac{1}{8}$".) Then, on the band saw, cut away the waste to separate the two tenons on each end of each apron section.

The tenons should come off of the table saw a little thicker than needed so you have some material to plane away when achieving the final fit. Fit each tenon to each mortise.

The screw pockets on the inside of the apron should be cut before you assemble the table. These can be made on the drill press using a Forstner bit, but I decided to use chisels and gouges as the Pleasant Hill maker had done.

I started by drawing lines on the inside face of the apron sections 1" from the top edge. I then made two marks along each of these lines 1" from the shoulders. I used the intersection of these marks as the center points for 1" in diameter half circles I inscribed with a compass. I used a paring chisel to cut the flat area at the top of each pocket. This flat was tilted about 70 degrees from the outside surface of the apron. I made the round half circle with a couple of carving gouges. You don't need to get fancy with these pockets. The ones on the original table were pretty crudely executed, probably because that craftsman knew they would never be seen by anyone except a nosy furniture maker like me.

Finish each pocket by drilling a through $\frac{3}{16}$" hole in the center of each pocket's flat spot. This hole should be at an angle about 90 degrees from the surface of the pocket's flat. This will create an angle that does two things. First, it will keep the hole from breaking out on the outside face of the apron section. Second, it will allow you to use 2" #6 drywall screws (coarse threaded) to hold the $\frac{7}{8}$" thick top in place without breaking through the top.

Split out the pegs. Then shave them to size with a paring chisel.

## Gluing It Up

I undercut by $\frac{1}{8}$" the middle edges of each tenon (the edges adjacent to the waste you removed between the tenons). This provides a little breathing room if the apron begins to shrink across its width.

Then swab a little glue into each mortise and on each tenon and assemble the base of the table, seating each tenon under pressure from a bar or pipe clamp. (It might be helpful to have an assistant as you do this because you'll be joining eight pieces of material all at the same time.)

Once the tenons have been seated, check the frame for square (when viewed from above). This is best done by measuring the diagonals of the frame. If the measurements aren't identical, apply a little pressure along the longer diagonal. This will cause a very slight racking of the case, bringing the frame into alignment.

Each tenon is then further secured via a round peg tapped into a drilled hole that passes through the post and through the tenon.

These pegs are best made by hand. Begin by cutting a one inch long section of material of the same species as the table. Then with a wide chisel, split (rive) peg blanks that are approximately $\frac{3}{8}$" on a side. Then, standing the peg blanks on end, carefully shave each one with a sharp paring chisel down to an approximately round shape, about $\frac{1}{4}$" in diameter. This is best done by working toward both ends from the middle of the peg. The pegs should taper from a diameter of a bit less than $\frac{1}{4}$" on one end to a bit more than $\frac{1}{4}$" on the other end.

The peg holes on the original were bored, I suspect, without measuring because there was a fair amount of variation in their placement. I bored mine in measured locations, $\frac{1}{2}$" from the tenon shoulder and $\frac{3}{4}$" from the top and bottom of each apron section

Put a dab of glue on the thinner end of your peg and tap the peg, thinner end first, into the hole.

The peg holes on the original were bored clear through the post so that one end of the peg pokes through on the inside. I decided that mine would go in only $\frac{7}{8}$". That would be deep enough to penetrate the apron and would then leave me with about $\frac{1}{8}$" to plane off on the outside of the post. After the pegs have been installed, plane the ends flush with the post.

Invert the top on your bench, protecting it with a towel or blanket. Then center the undercarriage and join the two parts with eight 2" #6 drywall screws. Sand and finish to suit.

# Sconce

MATERIAL: *cherry, tin*
LOCATION: *cellar, Centre Family Dwelling*

This is very similar to a Pleasant Hill sconce that appeared in John Kassay's seminal work *The Book of Shaker Furniture*. The top of the backing board on the sconce in Kassay's book comes to a point with an arcing slope on either side. The corners at the top of the backing board on this sconce are simply nipped away at an approximately 45 degree angle.

Like so many objects of Shaker woodenware, this sconce (and the one in Kassay) is designed to make use of the ubiquitous peg (or pin) board found in nearly every room of nearly every Shaker building. The sconce is hung on the wall by placing one of the holes in its backing board over a peg.

Notice that the drawing indicates the holes on the backing board are not equally spaced. As the sconce is lowered closer to a level that would permit someone to read by the candle's light, the peg holes are more closely spaced. While this could be the result of a workshop miscalculation, it might also represent a way to fine tune the amount of usable light given off by the candle.

**LEFT** In the 19th-century, before electric lights had been wired into every American home, rooms were lit with lanterns or candles. This cleverly designed sconce was created to hold a single candle at a height that would allow its illumination to spread across an entire room.

**RIGHT** The height at which the sconce was hung could be changed through the use of these peg holes.

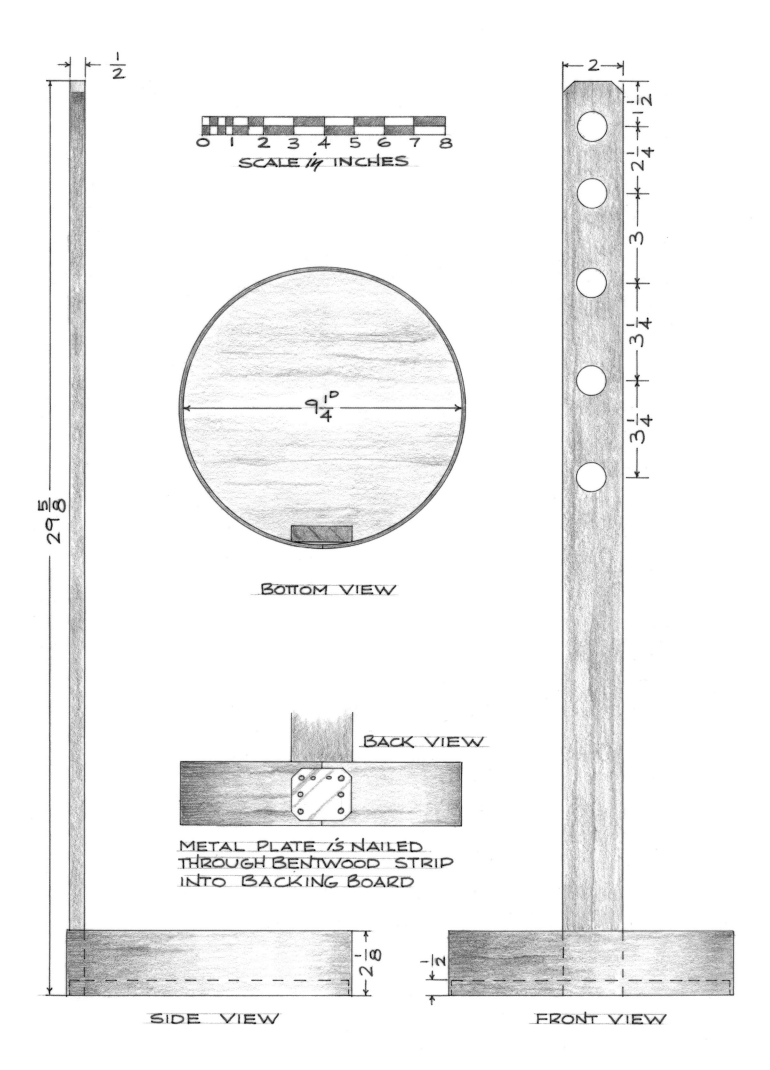

$\frac{1}{2}$

0 1 2 3 4 5 6 7 8
SCALE *in* INCHES

$9\frac{1}{4}^D$

BOTTOM VIEW

$29\frac{5}{8}$

BACK VIEW

METAL PLATE *is* NAILED
THROUGH BENTWOOD STRIP
INTO BACKING BOARD

2

$\frac{1}{2}$

$2\frac{1}{4}$

3

$3\frac{1}{4}$

$3\frac{1}{4}$

$2\frac{1}{8}$

$\frac{1}{2}$

SIDE VIEW

FRONT VIEW

A bentwood strip intended to hold any wax that might escape
the metal candleholder surrounds the wooden sconce bottom.

# Curly Cherry Secretary

MATERIAL: *cherry, poplar, fruitwood(?), brass*
LOCATION: *second floor, Meeting House*

I wanted this book to include at least one Pleasant Hill piece that could be considered a masterpiece, and I came away from my first trip to Pleasant Hill with two candidates for this position. One was a towering cupboard-over chest-of-drawers signed and dated "Charles Hamlin 1877". That piece (upper photo page 56) has the size and gravitas one expects from a piece given the masterpiece designation.

This curly cherry secretary does as well. But this secretary is also flawed, blemished in a way that gives a human touch to the hand (or hands) that created it.

When you enter the second-floor room of the Pleasant Hill Meeting House in which this piece is housed, your first reaction is likely to include an awareness of the secretary's size and its striking curly figure.

Curly cherry is a moderately rare variety of cherry.

**LEFT** This stately and austere masterpiece is one of the finest known examples of Pleasant Hill cabinetmaking. Notice the heavily figured material used to frame the upper doors. Notice also the alternating directions of the bands of curly figure on the drawer fronts.

**ABOVE** The top drawer front is hinged so that it can be lowered to become the writing surface for a concealed desk that includes four small drawers, a central compartment with a door that features a key lock, and eight cubbyholes.

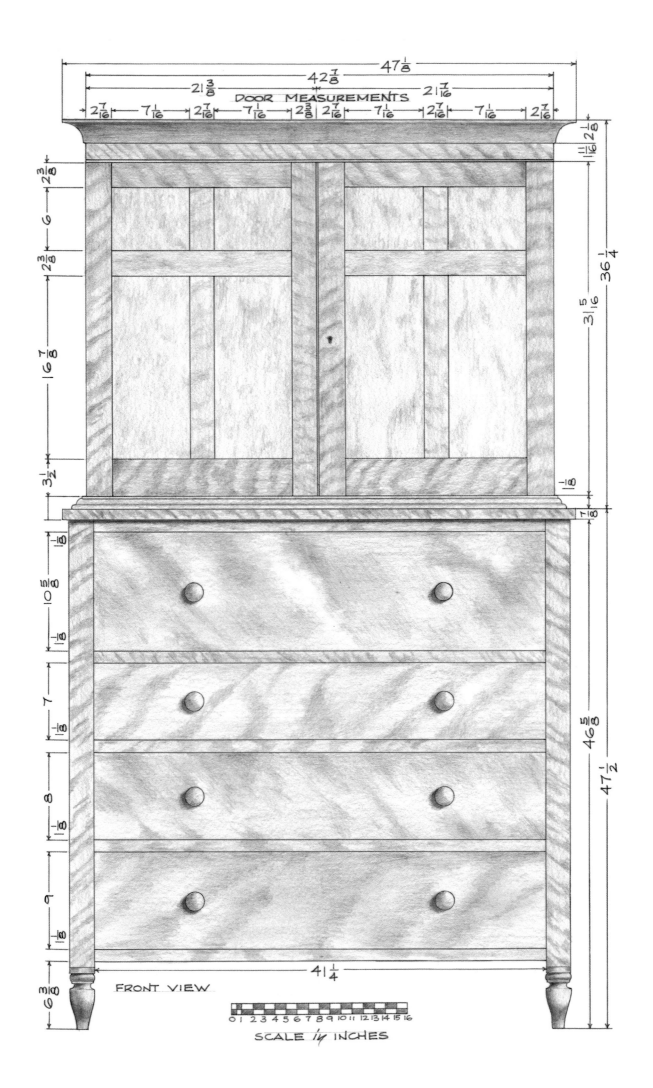

DOOR MEASUREMENTS

FRONT VIEW

SCALE 1/4 INCHES

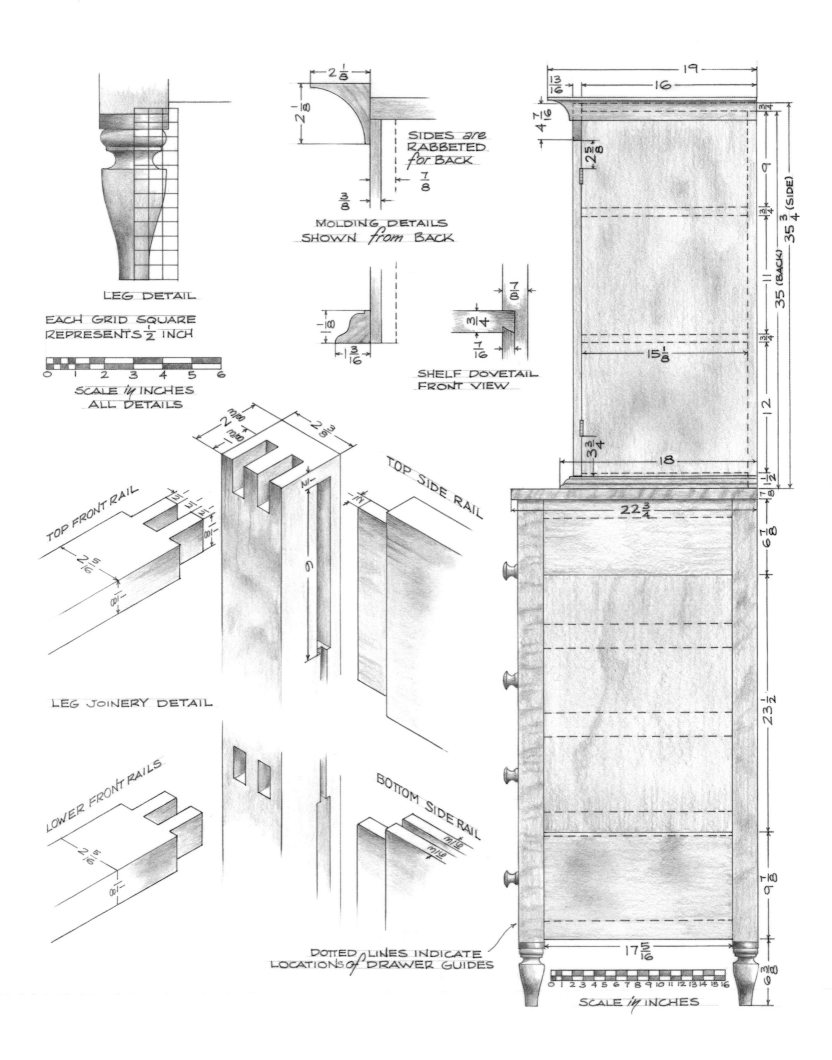

**LEG DETAIL**

EACH GRID SQUARE
REPRESENTS ½ INCH

SCALE in INCHES
ALL DETAILS

**LEG JOINERY DETAIL**

TOP FRONT RAIL

LOWER FRONT RAILS

SIDES *are*
RABBETED
*for* BACK

MOLDING DETAILS
SHOWN *from* BACK

SHELF DOVETAIL
FRONT VIEW

TOP SIDE RAIL

BOTTOM SIDE RAIL

DOTTED LINES INDICATE
LOCATIONS *of* DRAWER GUIDES

SCALE in INCHES

The upper case is surmounted with a wide crown molding typical of large Pleasant Hill casepieces.

Many trees will yield a board or two with patches of curly figure much like that visible in this secretary, but few trees will yield a whole log's worth as was the case, I believe, with the single tree which supplied the wood for this piece. I suspect that the sawyer (possibly Shaker) who opened up this log saw what he had, and, after cutting the log to get maximum yield, stickered the material and set it aside. ("Stickering" is the process of stacking green lumber with sticks placed perpendicular to every layer of freshly sawn boards so that air can circulate through the stack to dry the material.) Then a couple of years or a couple of decades later, a Shaker craftsman set to work with this material and began building this curly cherry cupboard over chest of drawers that would be his monument to the cabinetmaking craft.

The chest of drawers is built in the same way as many other Pleasant Hill chests of drawers from the middle decades of the 19th century. A post at each corner runs up from a turned foot at the floor to the underside of the chest top. Wide rails are mortised into the posts at the top and bottom of each end. A floating panel then rides in a groove cut into the inside edges of the rails and posts. While the mortise-and-tenon joinery connecting rails and posts is glued, the central panel is unglued to allow for expansion and contraction across its width.

The cupboard top is a separate unit which sits on top of the chest bottom. The two frame-and-panel doors of this cupboard top are hinged on the back of the outside stiles into the front edge of the cupboard sides. A wide cove molding, similar to crown moldings on other Pleasant Hill pieces, surmounts the cupboard.

Evidence of the maker's skills can be seen in the pleasing overall proportions of this masterpiece and in the competence he brought to the execution of each of its parts. Further evidence can be found in the manner in which the craftsman made use of the magnificent curly cherry.

He was careful to frame the doors of the upper unit using the secretary's most heavily figured stock. Notice that the middle stiles (and rails) are much less heavily figured than the components that make up the outer rails and stiles. This curly cherry perimeter serves to keep the eye from wandering away from the piece. (Rails are the horizontal frame components in a frame-and-panel door. Stiles are the vertical frame components.)

Notice also the adept handling of figured material in the four drawer fronts. Each drawer front is cut from a curly cherry board in a way that causes the bands of curl to march across the front at a consistent 45 degree angle. Notice the way he has alternated these marching bands of curl. The curl in the bottom drawer rises to the right. The curl in the next drawer up rises to the left. The curl in the next drawer rises once again to the right. And finally, the curl in the top drawer rises once again to the left. This controlled use of figured material is something often found in high-style period work on the eastern seaboard but not often in country work in the American interior.

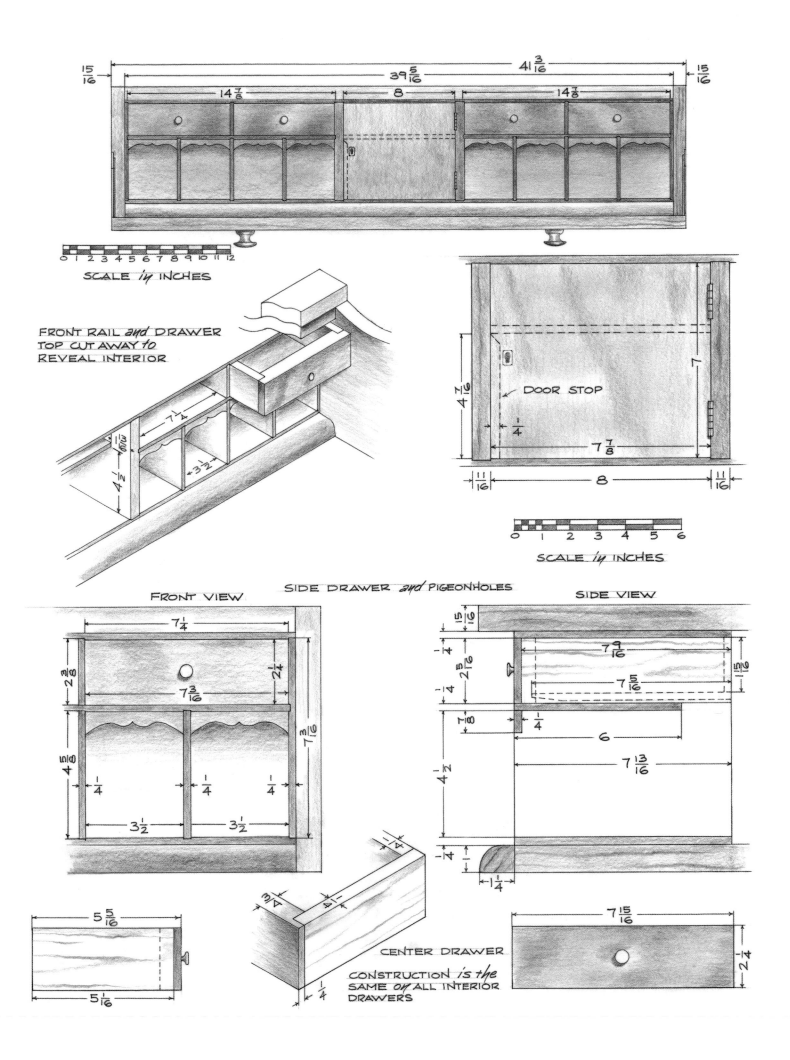

15/16

41 3/16

39 5/16

15/16

14 7/8

8

14 7/8

0 1 2 3 4 5 6 7 8 9 10 11 12

SCALE 1/4 INCHES

FRONT RAIL *and* DRAWER
TOP CUT AWAY *to*
REVEAL INTERIOR

7 1/4

3/16

4 1/2

3 1/2

DOOR STOP

4 7/16

7

1/4

7 7/8

11/16

8

11/16

0 1 2 3 4 5 6

SCALE 1/4 INCHES

SIDE DRAWER *and* PIGEONHOLES

FRONT VIEW

SIDE VIEW

7 1/4

2 3/8

2 1/4

7 3/16

7 3/16

4 5/8

1/4

1/4

1/4

3 1/2

3 1/2

15/16

1/4

2 5/16

1/4

7 9/16

7 5/16

15/16

7/8

1/4

6

4 1/2

7 13/16

1/4

1

1 1/4

5 5/16

5 1/16

3/4

1/4

1/4

CENTER DRAWER

CONSTRUCTION *is the*
SAME *on* ALL INTERIOR
DRAWERS

1/4

7 15/16

2 1/4

The floating panels on the upper compartment have beveled edges so that they can be
fit into grooves cut in the inside edges of the doors' rails and stiles.

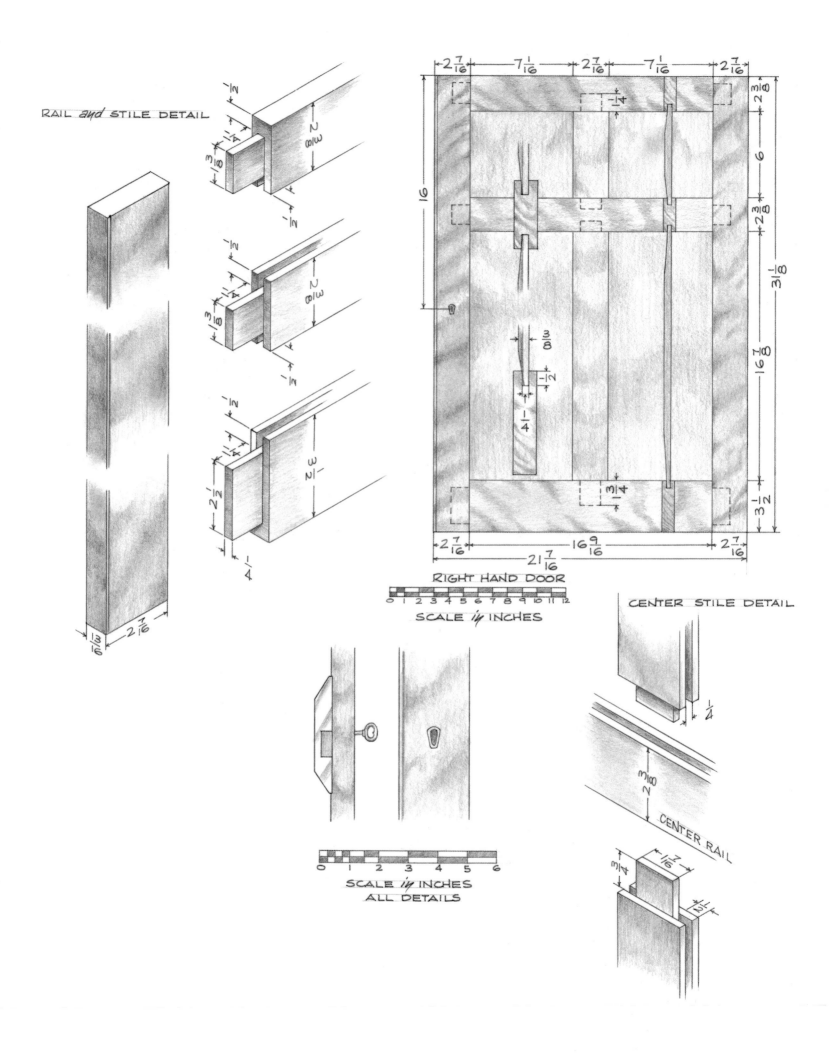

RAIL *and* STILE DETAIL

RIGHT HAND DOOR

SCALE *in* INCHES

CENTER STILE DETAIL

CENTER RAIL

SCALE *in* INCHES
ALL DETAILS

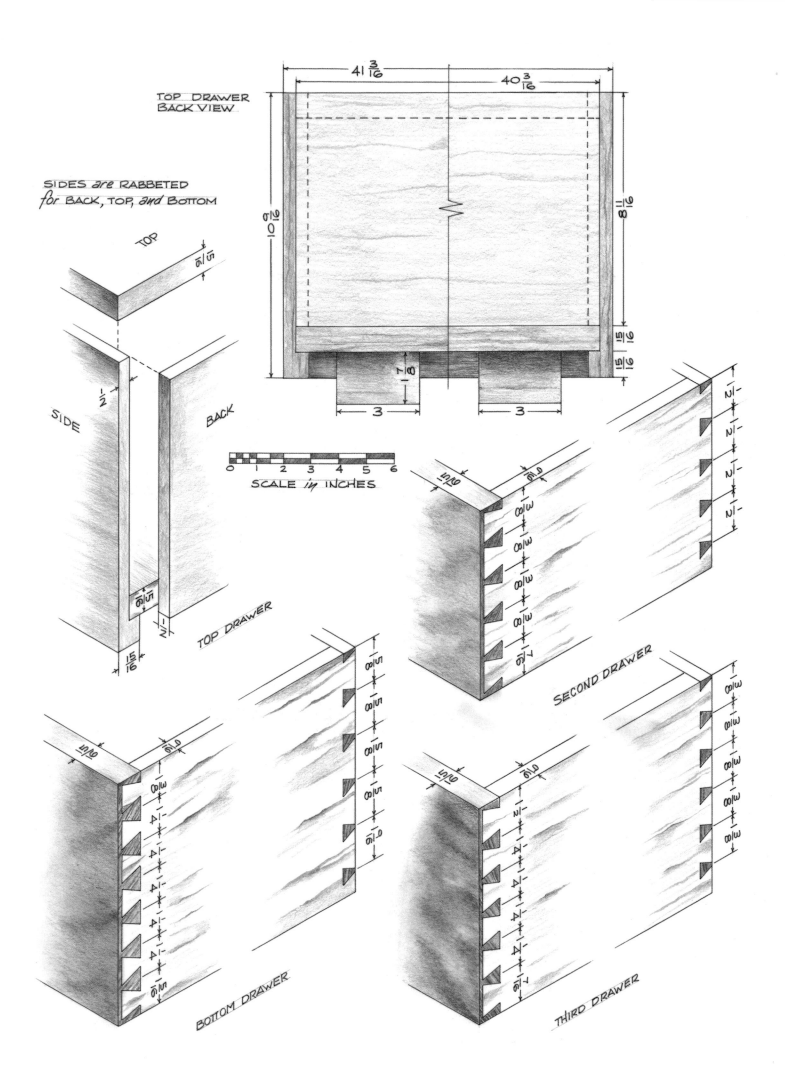

TOP DRAWER
BACK VIEW

SIDES *are* RABBETED
*for* BACK, TOP, *and* BOTTOM

TOP

SIDE

BACK

$41\frac{3}{16}$

$40\frac{3}{16}$

$10\frac{9}{16}$

$8\frac{11}{16}$

$\frac{15}{16}$

$\frac{15}{16}$

$1\frac{7}{8}$

3

3

$\frac{1}{2}$

$\frac{5}{16}$

$\frac{5}{16}$

$\frac{1}{2}$

$\frac{15}{16}$

0  1  2  3  4  5  6
SCALE *in* INCHES

TOP DRAWER

$\frac{9}{16}$

$\frac{5}{16}$

$\frac{3}{8}$
$\frac{3}{8}$
$\frac{3}{8}$
$\frac{3}{8}$
$\frac{7}{16}$

$\frac{1}{2}$
$\frac{1}{2}$
$\frac{1}{2}$
$\frac{1}{2}$
$\frac{1}{2}$

SECOND DRAWER

$\frac{9}{16}$

$\frac{5}{16}$

$\frac{3}{8}$
$\frac{1}{4}$
$\frac{1}{4}$
$\frac{1}{4}$
$\frac{1}{4}$
$\frac{7}{16}$

$\frac{5}{16}$
$\frac{5}{16}$
$\frac{5}{16}$
$\frac{5}{16}$
$\frac{7}{16}$

BOTTOM DRAWER

$\frac{9}{16}$

$\frac{5}{16}$

$\frac{3}{8}$
$\frac{1}{4}$
$\frac{1}{4}$
$\frac{1}{4}$
$\frac{7}{16}$

$\frac{3}{8}$
$\frac{3}{8}$
$\frac{3}{8}$
$\frac{3}{8}$
$\frac{3}{8}$

THIRD DRAWER

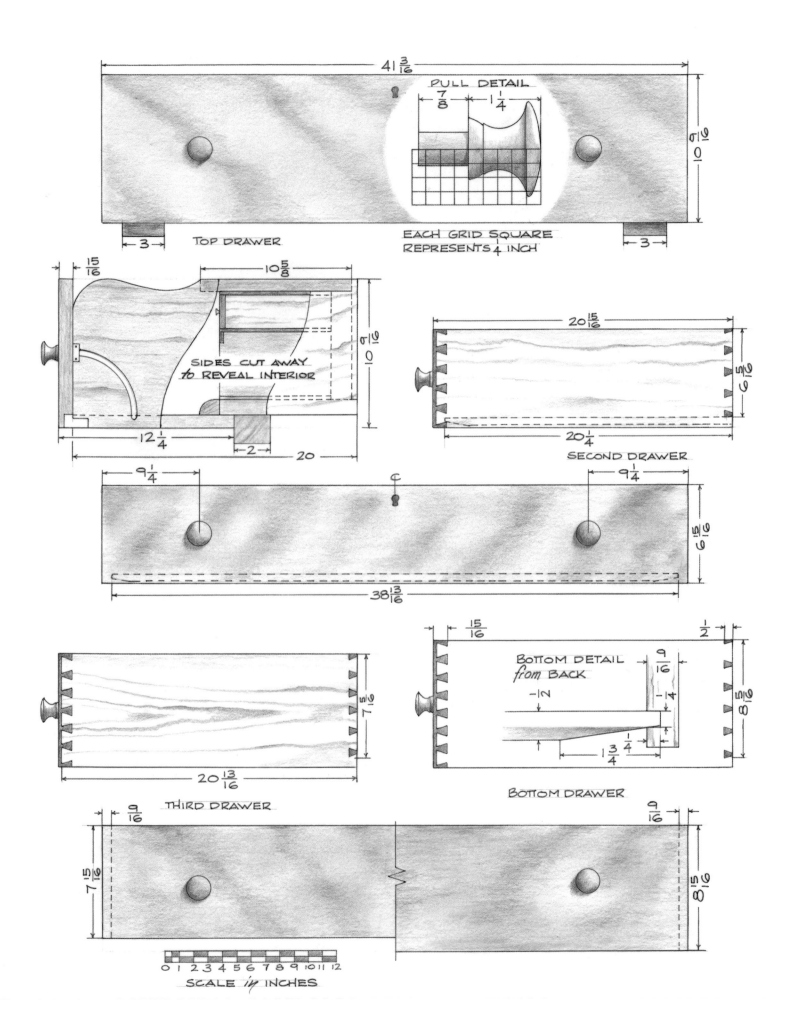

41 3/16

9 10/16

PULL DETAIL

7/8     1 1/4

3     TOP DRAWER     3

EACH GRID SQUARE
REPRESENTS 1/4 INCH

15/16

10 5/8

9 10/16

SIDES CUT AWAY
to REVEAL INTERIOR

12 1/4     2     20

20 15/16

6 5/16

20 1/4

SECOND DRAWER

9 1/4     C     9 1/4

6 15/16

38 13/16

7 5/16

20 13/16

THIRD DRAWER

15/16     1/2

BOTTOM DETAIL
from BACK

9/16

1/4

1/2

1 3/4     1/4

8 5/16

BOTTOM DRAWER

9/16     9/16

7 15/16     8 15/16

0 1 2 3 4 5 6 7 8 9 10 11 12
SCALE in INCHES

Because it exhibits a consistently high standard of design and construction excellence, this work was all done, I believe, by the same highly competent craftsman, probably at the same time.

The desk, however, is another matter.

Like many secretaries of the era, the writing surface of this secretary is created when the false front of the top drawer is opened and locked into place parallel to the floor. I don't believe this is a feature that the cupboard-on-chest-of-drawers has had since its creation. A close examination of the end grain surfaces on the drawer front reveals vestigial dovetail sockets filled now with bits of stained or painted wood. This suggests that what is now a drop front was once a drawer.

But even more telling than the evidence of filled dovetail sockets is the difference in quality apparent in those elements making up the desk. The long quarter-circle mortises which house the lid stays on the outsides of the desk unit were crudely formed by someone with only rudimentary skills. Plus the tiny drawers at the rear of the desk's interior are assembled with simple nails, rather than the dovetails employed by the original maker for the large drawers below. But the clumsiest work in the entire piece can be seen when you line up the tiny cubbyhole drawers side by side and look down on them. Despite the fact that each is fit into an opening of the same length, each drawer has a significantly different front-to-back measurement. To compensate for this variation, the maker of this desk unit tacked bits of scrap to the backs of the shortest drawers, so that when they

Detail of the drop front.

are closed, the fronts are all properly aligned. My guess is that he made mistakes when cutting the drawer sides to length and rather than cut new sides to the right length, he chose to add the bits of scrap to the backs of the drawers thinking that no one would ever know.

Finally there is one more feature of this desk that needs discussion, and that is its design. When you study my brother's drawings for the desk interior what you see is a very pleasing arrangement of shapes. A wide center cubbyhole is flanked by two pairs of smaller cubbyholes on each side, setting up a strong rhythm as the eye moves across the desk unit. There is a bit of scrollwork at the top of the flanking cubbyholes which adds an appealing visual detail. Together, these elements suggest a professional design, one perhaps beyond the reach of the craftsman who did the work. It's possible, therefore, that the workman who executed the desk was working from another source, from perhaps a published source in one of the many magazines that came into existence in the second half of the 19th century or from perhaps a professionally made desk he had seen somewhere.

Despite my criticism of the workmanship of the secretary's desk unit, I believe that the unit adds immeasurably to the appeal of this piece. In fact, perhaps strangely, without that poorly executed addition, I'm not sure I would have identified this piece as a Pleasant Hill masterpiece.

# Hanging Cupboard

MATERIAL: *poplar, brass*

LOCATION: *infirmary, second floor, Centre Family Dwelling*

### Reproducing the Hanging Cupboard

I began my study of the Shaker furniture at Pleasant Hill, Kentucky, with a quick survey of the contents of the enormous Centre Family Dwelling, sticking my head in the door of each room, making a mental note of everything that caught my eye: a table here, a chair there, a little blanket chest, a tripled clothes hanger. Each of the items on this mental list had something about it that set it apart from the other objects in the Dwelling. In some cases, it was a splash of color, in others a bit of intriguing joinery, in others a form that deviated in some way from Shaker norms. In this manner, I chugged along for maybe half an hour, looking, storing, excited about the prospect of looking even more closely later on.

Then in a small room on the second floor, I saw this cupboard hanging from a peg rail above a wash stand.

**ABOVE** The original cupboard had been dyed or stained to permit some of the poplar figure to show through. This finish had darkened over time. In an effort to approximate that darkened color, I painted my reproduction.

**LEFT** Much Pleasant Hill utilitarian furniture—like this cupboard—was made of poplar, a soft, easily worked native hardwood.

I stuck my head in, caught my breath, released it, then slowly entered the room. The cupboard was familiar. Maybe it was from Christian Becksvoort's book. But I had forgotten about it. I know I wasn't expecting to see it there.

I stepped over the low railing erected to keep the public at a distance. I stuck my nose up close to the piece to study the pegs that penetrated the joinery of the frame-and-panel door, then backed off. This was something special, something profoundly Shaker, something that, unlike many pieces in the Pleasant Hill collection, could never be attributed to country origins.

### Material

I usually buy my lumber from hardwood dealers. These are businesses that typically require a 100 board feet. minimum order and typically sell only in 100 bf. increments. So I can't buy just 75 bf. of curly maple for example.

In most cases, I don't mind these minimums. I always need cherry and walnut and curly maple. But sometimes, I don't really want a 100 bf. of a particular species, and anyone buying small lots of hardwood at stores catering to woodworking hobbyists needs the support of a full-time cardiologist.

Recently, I've been experimenting with another source for poplar: home improvement centers. They charge more per board foot than a hardwood dealer but there are, I believe, some good reasons to consider them, at least for poplar.

For one thing, home improvement centers offer material that has already been surfaced. Let's face it: one of the more odious woodshop chores is flattening and thicknessing material before you start a project. But here's a more important reason: At home improvement centers, I only buy perfect boards. If there's a knot, a split, a bit of wane, I don't buy it. If it's not perfectly flat—and I do mean billiard table flat—I put it back.

Try that with a hardwood dealer. Yes, he might let you set aside a few boards with some really egregious defects, but if you reject eight boards out of ten, he might

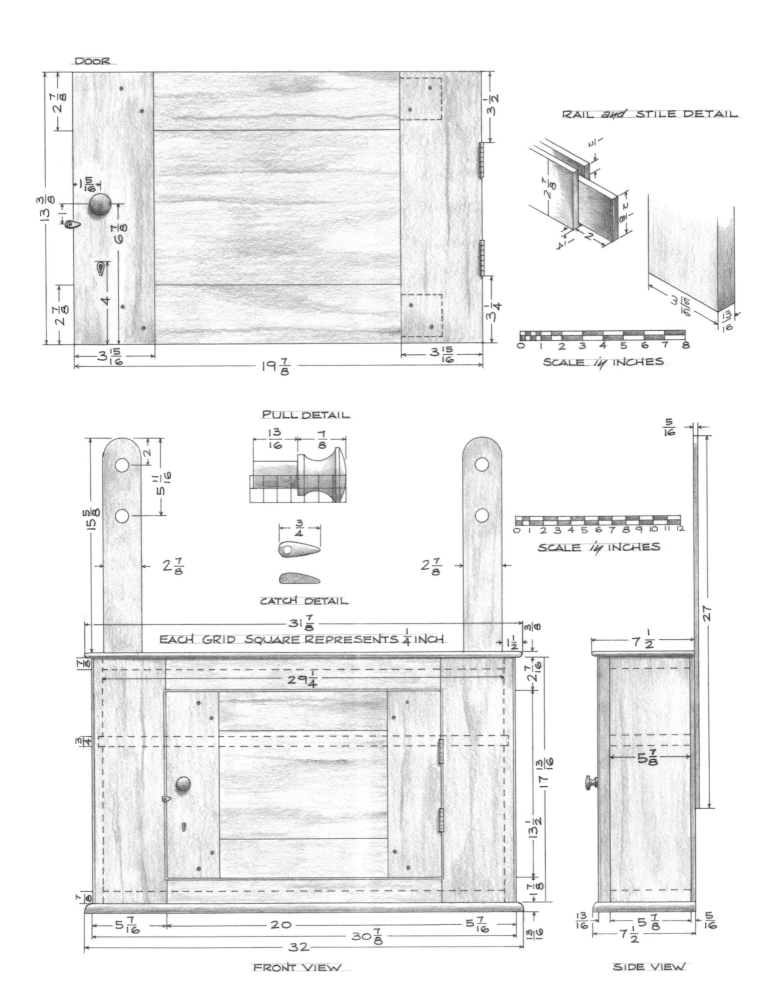

DOOR

$2\frac{7}{8}$

$\frac{1}{2}$

$3\frac{1}{2}$

$13\frac{3}{8}$

$\frac{1}{16} \times 1\frac{5}{16}$

$6\frac{7}{8}$

$2\frac{7}{8}$

4

$3\frac{1}{4}$

$3\frac{15}{16}$

$3\frac{15}{16}$

$19\frac{7}{8}$

RAIL and STILE DETAIL

$\frac{1}{3}$

$2\frac{7}{8}$

$1\frac{3}{8}$

$\frac{1}{4}$   2

$\frac{15}{16}$   $\frac{13}{16}$

SCALE in INCHES

0 1 2 3 4 5 6 7 8

PULL DETAIL

$\frac{13}{16}$   $\frac{7}{8}$

$\frac{3}{4}$

CATCH DETAIL

2

$5\frac{11}{16}$

$15\frac{5}{8}$

$2\frac{7}{8}$

$2\frac{7}{8}$

$\frac{3}{8}$

$1\frac{1}{2}$

$31\frac{7}{8}$

EACH GRID SQUARE REPRESENTS $\frac{1}{4}$ INCH

$29\frac{1}{4}$

$\frac{7}{8}$

$\frac{3}{4}$

$2\frac{7}{16}$

$17\frac{13}{16}$

$13\frac{1}{2}$

$1\frac{7}{8}$

$\frac{7}{8}$

$5\frac{7}{16}$   20   $5\frac{7}{16}$

$30\frac{7}{8}$

$\frac{13}{16}$

32

FRONT VIEW

$\frac{5}{16}$

SCALE in INCHES

0 1 2 3 4 5 6 7 8 9 10 11 12

$7\frac{1}{2}$

27

$5\frac{7}{8}$

$\frac{13}{16}$   $5\frac{7}{8}$   $\frac{5}{16}$

$7\frac{1}{2}$

SIDE VIEW

decide he doesn't want your business after all.

In fact, I have developed the habit of buying all my secondary wood this way. Each time I go to a home improvement center, I sort through all the poplar and all the clear white pine and I buy every single perfect board I see.

This little cupboard is built of poplar I'd culled from the stock of my local home improvement center during the previous month.

## Assembling the Case

I chose to use 8d coated nails to assemble the cupboard because the nail heads visible on the original are about the size of 8d nail heads, and I knew 8d nails would result in a solid construction. Eight penny nails are big for this application, and I think you could have good results with a 7d nail as well, but I wouldn't recommend dropping any further on the size scale.

Initially, the whole nail thing made me uncomfortable. I've spent too many years cutting wood-to-wood joinery to embrace what seems to be a sacrilegious method of work. But early in the construction process, I had to remove a piece I'd nailed in the wrong location, and let's just say I'm convinced this little cupboard will never come apart.

These nails require the drilling of two holes. The first is a through hole in the board you're nailing through. This hole should be just large enough for the shank of an 8d penny nail to pass without being driven by your hammer. The second hole should be the full length of your 8d nail and just a bit smaller than the shank of the nail. It has to be small enough so that you have to drive the nail in with your hammer but not so small that seating the nail results in split material. As always, experiment on scrap before you work on the good stuff.

The top photo shows me drilling the smaller hole in a partially assembled joint. The drill for the larger, through hole, sits on the bench behind me.

After nailing the frame together, tap the shelf into its dadoes.

The original cupboard has only one shelf, although there are dadoes for two equally spaced shelves. I thought that an interior divided into only two compartments, instead of three, made more sense on this modest-sized cupboard, so I eliminated the second shelf the original cupboard had at birth. This gave me a fairly small compartment above and a larger compartment below.

After the shelf has been nailed into place, level the cabinet front and back with a plane.

The cupboard has ⅛" beads along each of the front corners and around the door frame. The beads on the corners are cut on both the front and side of the vertical

**TOP** Although it's possible to drive nails into "green" hardwood without pre-drilling, thoroughly dry hardwood requires pre-drilled holes—that is if you want to avoid split stock. The through hole should be nearly the same diameter as the shank of the nail. The hole that penetrates the second piece of stock should be a bit smaller in order to give the material a good grip on the nail.

**BOTTOM** Although the bead on the Shaker original was likely made with a scratch stock (since there is evidence of this tool everywhere at Pleasant Hill), I chose an ⅛" side bead plane.

parts of the cupboard front. This produces a bead that's visible from either perspective.

## Using Hand Planes

If you haven't used a molding plane, an ⅛" side bead plane like the one I'm using in the lower photo is a great place to start. You can find these relatively common planes at flea markets, antique malls and on eBay, of course. But you must be sure to purchase a plane with a reasonably straight sole. Some have bowed beyond repair in the century and a half since their creation. "Reasonably" straight, however, doesn't mean "perfectly" straight. This little ⅛" side-bead plane I'm using here has a bit of a bow but it still works fine.

Unlike most molding planes, which are designed to be held at an angle (the spring angle), side bead planes are designed to be held upright, their sides perpendicular to the surfaces being worked. Set the iron so that it's barely visible when you sight along the sole of the plane, tap the wedge firm, then crowd the plane's fence against the edge of the work and push the plane forward. If you have the right amount of iron exposed, a tiny shaving will squirt out the side of the plane. (Test the plane's setting on scrap before working on the cupboard stock. A rank iron, one set too deep, can tear out the bead.) After a half dozen passes, you will have defined a neat little bead and quirk.

If you prefer routers, there are $1/8"$ bead cutters available that will simulate the work of this plane.

Cutting the bead around the door on the vertical parts of the cupboard front requires a little trickery because you simply can't do it with a properly set up side bead plane. This is because the bead doesn't run all the way to the ends of the boards on the vertical front components (although the bead does run from end to end on the horizontal front components so these beads can be cut in the way I'm demonstrating in the lower photo on the previous page).

**TOP** The junction of the horizontal and vertical beads must be completed with a little paring-chisel work.

**BOTTOM** Bench planes can be made to do a fair amount of edge shaping. Here, I'm using a bench plane to create a radius between a line drawn on the edge and a line drawn on the top of the cupboard bottom.

The Shaker maker might have done this with a scratch stock. See pages 47 and 48 in Chapter 5 for a discussion of scratch stocks.

You can, however, cut the stopped bead on the vertical components of the cabinet front with a side bead plane if you cheat a little. Tap the iron down so that it hangs an extra $1/8"$ or so from the sole of the plane. That will allow the iron to engage the work when the sole of the plane is not riding down on the bead you're cutting. You are, in effect, using the side bead plane as a beading tool. This too is something you should experiment with on scrap before trying it out on the good stuff.

After the frame has been assembled, you'll then finish the bead around the door with a paring chisel as shown in the top photo, followed by sandpaper.

Nail the components of the door frame.

The cupboard top and bottom both have radiussed edges on their fronts and ends.. The top has a 180 degree radius, the bottom only a 90 degree radius. These radii can be formed with molding planes (or roundover bits in a router), but I've always made this shape with a bench plane. You'll be amazed at how quickly you can do this work—in much less time than it would take you to set up a router to perform the same operation, and of course working with a plane means no dust and no noise. The shop remains quiet enough to plan the next few steps in the construction process.

If you choose my method, you'll first need some pencil lines to plane between. One of these lines should identify the midpoint of the board's edge. The other should be placed on an adjacent surface a distance from the edge equal to half the thickness of the board. In other words, you will scribe two lines on adjacent surfaces, each of which is the same distance from the same corner. If you look closely at the photo above, you'll be able to see the guidelines I drew.

To create the radius, simply remove shavings in the area between these lines until you've established the rounded edge.

You should create the radii on the ends of the board before tackling the long-grain radius. This is because creating the end-grain radius may lift some wood fibers from the adjacent long-grain edge. If, however, you begin with the ends, any long-grain fibers you dislodge will likely be a part of the waste you'll later remove when you create the radius on the long-grain edge of the board. In addition, you should use a paring chisel to create a little bevel on the corner before working the end grain with your plane. This gives you additional protection from breaking out long-grain wood fibers at the ends of the plane strokes on the end grain. Of course, you must remember to work your plane from the back side of the end grain radii toward the front so that you won't dislodge any long-grain fibers on the back edge. Finish the radii with sandpaper.

## Making the Door

The cabinet took me maybe three hours to assemble. The door took a day and a half to build and fit. In part, this is because the door is the only element with any traditional joinery, but primarily, it was because doors require a lot of careful fitting.

The original door has 2"-wide, $1/4$"-thick, 4"-long through tenons on the rails which fit through 2"-wide, $1/4$"-thick, 4"-long mortises in the stiles.

So did the first door I made for this reproduction.

But the mortises must have been a little out of whack because when I assembled the door, it had an unacceptable amount of twist, a result probably of an incorrectly cut mortise. This is something that's very easy to do when you're chopping these very long and very thin mortises by hand. So I made a second door, this time with mortises only 2" deep. These were much easier to cut accurately, and a tightly fit 2"-long tenon has more than enough glue surface for this door, particularly when the glue joints are reinforced with $1/4$" walnut pegs.

The top photo shows the door components before the door was glued up. Notice the $1/4$"-wide, $1/2$"-deep through grooves milled into the inside edges of the door rails and stiles. The $1/4$"-thick center panel—which is not raised on either side—floats in these grooves.

The door is opened with a turned walnut knob. I turned two knobs from this spindle because I had decided to make a pair of these hanging cupboards.

The final touches on the door are the $1/4$" diameter pegs which reinforce each tenon. See the discussion of peg forming on page 75.

## Finishing

The original cupboard was stained red, but I opted for paint in order to better conceal the nail heads. I began with a coat of latex primer, which I sanded, then followed that with two coats of a designer red that approximated the color of the original piece.

The problem with paint is the dimensional change it causes. Each layer of paint adds measurably to the width and thickness of the part to which it's applied. A door stile that was 4" wide after sanding, might be $4^{1}/_{8}$" wide after applying three coats of paint, so even though I had fit the door with a comfortable $1/16$" gap all around, after painting I had to remove the door. In order to get the door to open and close properly I planed additional width from all the rails and stiles and then repainted those planed edges .

My wife asked me how the Shakers might have used the original cupboard. I had to tell her I didn't know.

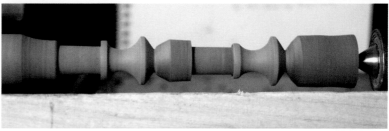

**TOP** Before you glue up the door, lay out the parts and make certain that they will all come together during glue-up.

**MIDDLE** Use a skew to shape the top of the knob and a fingernail gouge to cut the cove. The tenon can be cut with a paring chisel laid flat on the rest with the bevel down.

**BOTTOM** Riven pegs are not only historically accurate; they are also stronger than sawn pegs because they eliminate the possibility of grain run-out.

Because it was poplar, it probably was a utility cabinet of some kind that hung in a washroom to hold soaps or cleaning brushes. Because it was so portable, it probably had several incarnations in its original life, as the Shakers moved it from room to room to suit the needs of a community dwindling steadily in size.

My wife decided to hang hers in the kitchen and fill it with spices. The top surface will display her collection of antique tin cans with brightly lithographed color labels.

# Triple Hanger

MATERIAL: *cherry, leather*
LOCATION: *first floor, Centre Family Dwelling*

This unusual bit of woodenware is one of a pair, the other of which is in the hands of a private collector.

Each hanger is stamped with the initials "M. E. T.", which are believed to represent Mary Ellen Todd, who was born in Louisville, Kentucky, in 1844. She arrived at Pleasant Hill at age 7 and died there in 1881.

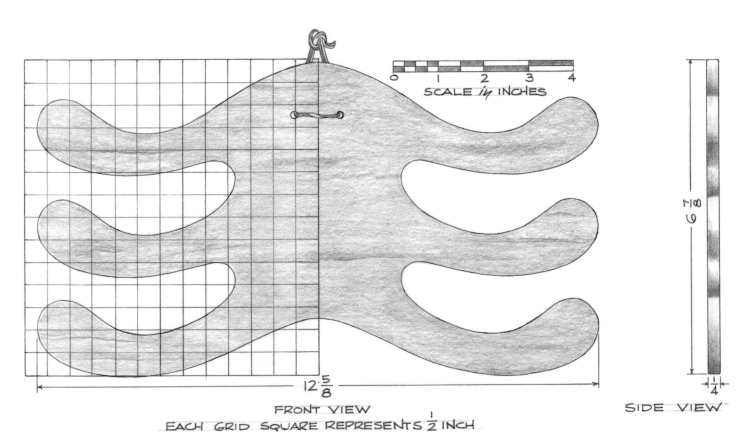

SCALE *in* INCHES

FRONT VIEW
EACH GRID SQUARE REPRESENTS $\frac{1}{2}$ INCH

SIDE VIEW

**LEFT** The Shakers made countless similar hangers, each consisting of a wood bar with what is usually a sensuous bandsawn profile. These were hung from pegs by leather thongs threaded through holes bored halfway along the lengths of the hangers. I've reproduced many of these, but I never saw a triple hanger until I came to Pleasant Hill.

# Side Table

MATERIAL: *walnut, yellow pine*
LOCATION: *second floor, Meeting House*

Like nearly all the Pleasant Hill tables I examined, the apron on this example is mortised into the legs. But unlike many others, this example has a rail above the drawer. Also unlike many other Pleasant Hill examples, this table was probably intended to be used only against a wall. The back apron section is pine rather than walnut like the apron sections on either end and the rails above and below the drawer.

Because of its width, this little walnut table was probably used as a desk, rather than a side table.

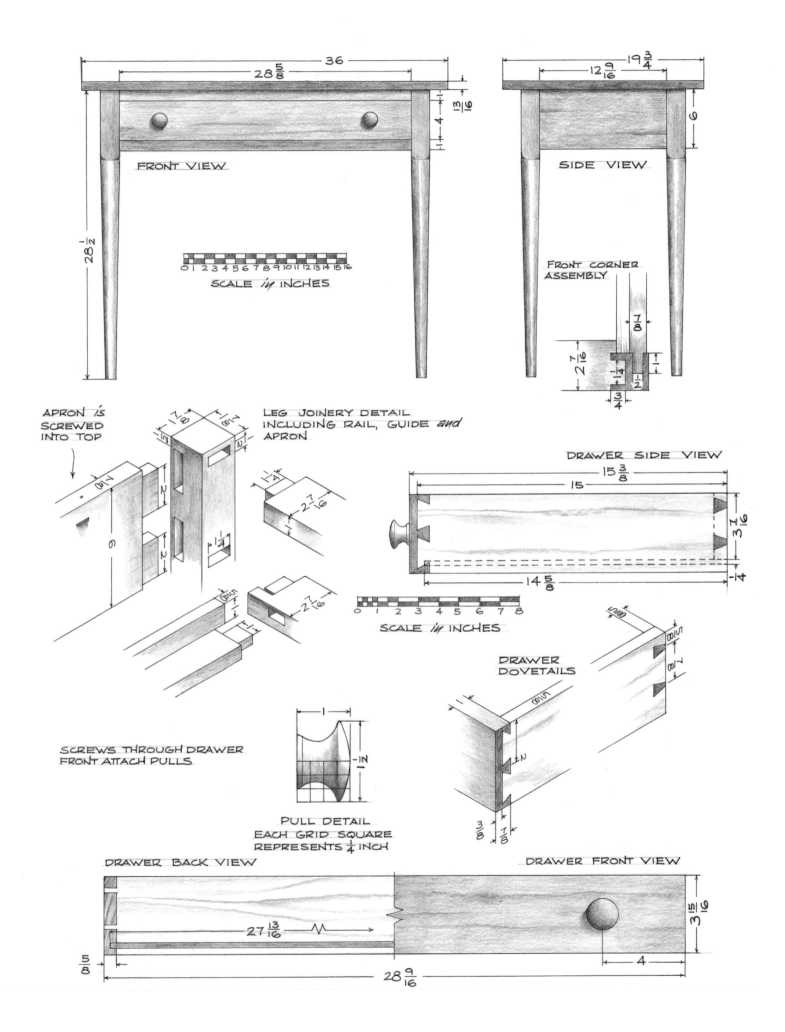

FRONT VIEW

36

28 5/8

28 1/2

13/16

1

4

SCALE in INCHES
0 1 2 3 4 5 6 7 8 9 10 11 12 13 14 15 16

SIDE VIEW

19 3/4

12 9/16

6

FRONT CORNER ASSEMBLY

7/8

2 7/16

1 1/4

1/2

1

3/4

APRON is SCREWED INTO TOP

LEG JOINERY DETAIL INCLUDING RAIL, GUIDE and APRON

7/8

1 1/4

1/2

6

2

2

1 1/4

2 7/16

1/4

1 1/4

1/2

2 7/16

DRAWER SIDE VIEW

15 3/8

15

14 5/8

3 1/4

1/4

SCALE in INCHES
0 1 2 3 4 5 6 7 8

DRAWER DOVETAILS

5/8

7/8

1

5/8

2

3/8

7/8

SCREWS THROUGH DRAWER FRONT ATTACH PULLS

1

1 1/2

PULL DETAIL
EACH GRID SQUARE REPRESENTS 1/4 INCH

DRAWER BACK VIEW

27 13/16

5/8

28 9/16

DRAWER FRONT VIEW

3 15/16

4

# Sewing Rocker

MATERIAL: *maple, hickory, Shaker tape (the original cane seat was replaced with Shaker tape in 1975)*
LOCATION: *Centre Family Dwelling, first floor*

A sewing rocker was built without arms so a Sister sitting in it would have no impediments to her arm motion as she worked.

The now badly faded Shaker tape seat (photo at right) is a replacement woven in 1975. This fading is characteristic of most modern Shaker tapes, particularly if they are exposed to natural light, as was the tape on this chair.

Post-and-rung chairmaking—at least as I practice it—requires some specialized jigs and fixtures. There wasn't room to present those jigs and fixtures in this book, but they can be found in another of my books: *Quick and Easy Jigs and Fixtures*, published by Popular Woodworking Books. My book *Authentic Shaker Furniture*, also published by Popular Woodworking Books, includes a more detailed discussion of my chairmaking practices.

## Build the Sewing Rocker

A rocking chair with four slats, bent back posts, and arms takes me about forty hours of shop time to build (although I'm sure a Pleasant Hill maker like Francis Montfort could have built a similar chair in less time). By contrast, this little armless, three-slat rocker with unbent back posts took no more than twenty-five hours to build.

## Materials

The original chair was made of a typical Pleasant Hill mix of materials: hard maple and probably hickory. Such a mix is found in nearly all of the Pleasant Hill chairs I examined. Posts were often made of hard maple, while the rungs and slats were fashioned from oak, hickory or ash. This mix of materials matches each species to the application for which each is best suited. Hard maple turns beautifully, so it's the perfect choice for a post that usually has a bit of turned ornamentation. Many ring porous woods like oak, ash and hickory are ridiculously strong when shaved down to a small diameter for rungs or when shaved to thinness for a slat, although their coarse

textures makes them less well suited for turned detail.

Unlike the Shaker who made this chair, modern makers like myself typically choose to use a single species for a particular chair because of the aesthetic coherence this approach produces. I have made chairs of white oak, ash, cherry, walnut and of course hard maple. But I rarely mix the materials in the same chair, and when I

**ABOVE** As you can see from the photo of my reproduction, I altered the shape of the top slat a little, giving it a little peak. No good reason. I just wanted to see what it would look like.

**LEFT** This petite rocker would be too small for most contemporary Americans, but it was appropriate for many of our smaller-framed ancestors.

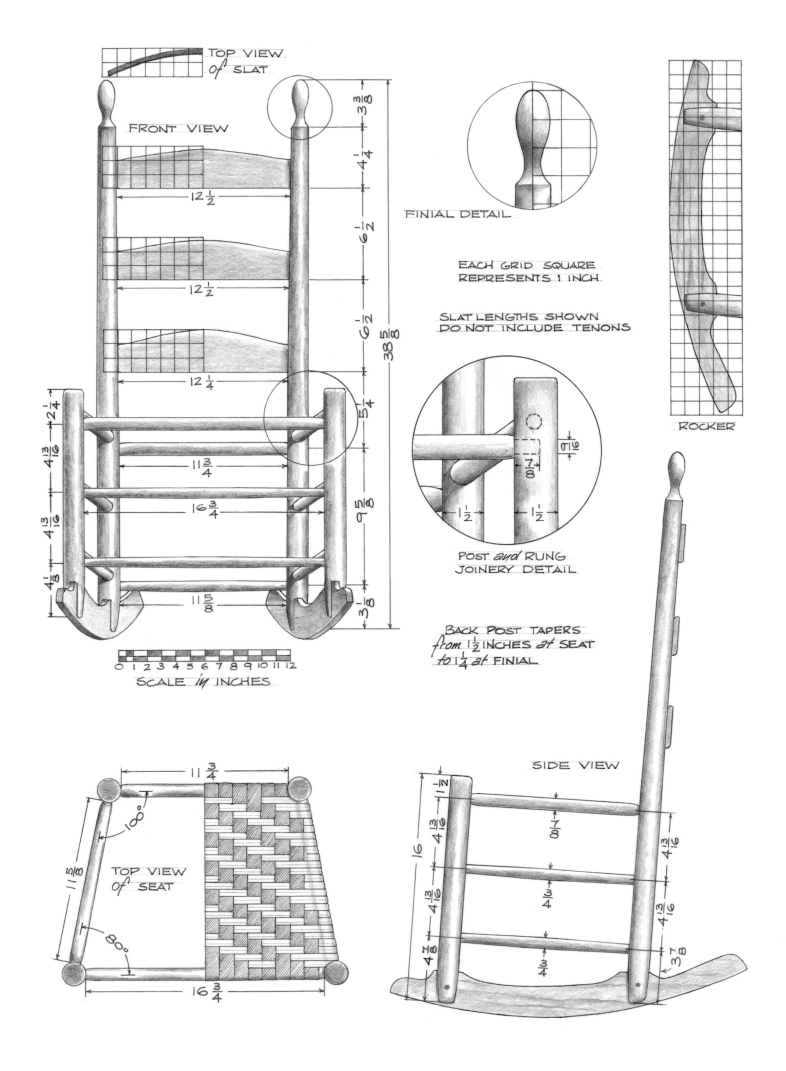

TOP VIEW of SLAT

FRONT VIEW

$12\frac{1}{2}$

$12\frac{1}{2}$

$12\frac{1}{4}$

$11\frac{3}{4}$

$16\frac{3}{4}$

$11\frac{5}{8}$

$2\frac{1}{4}$

$4\frac{13}{16}$

$4\frac{13}{16}$

$4\frac{13}{16}$

$4\frac{1}{8}$

$3\frac{3}{8}$

$4\frac{1}{4}$

$6\frac{1}{2}$

$6\frac{1}{2}$

$5\frac{1}{4}$

$9\frac{5}{8}$

$3\frac{1}{8}$

$38\frac{5}{8}$

0 1 2 3 4 5 6 7 8 9 10 11 12
SCALE *in* INCHES

FINIAL DETAIL

EACH GRID SQUARE
REPRESENTS 1 INCH

SLAT LENGTHS SHOWN
DO NOT INCLUDE TENONS

$\frac{9}{16}$

$\frac{7}{8}$

$1\frac{1}{2}$   $1\frac{1}{2}$

POST *and* RUNG
JOINERY DETAIL

BACK POST TAPERS
*from* $1\frac{1}{2}$ INCHES *at* SEAT
*to* $1\frac{1}{4}$ *at* FINIAL

ROCKER

SIDE VIEW

$1\frac{1}{2}$

$\frac{7}{8}$

16

$4\frac{13}{16}$

$4\frac{13}{16}$

$4\frac{13}{16}$

$4\frac{1}{8}$

$4\frac{13}{16}$

$\frac{3}{4}$

$\frac{3}{4}$

$3\frac{3}{8}$

TOP VIEW of SEAT

$11\frac{3}{4}$

$11\frac{5}{8}$

$16\frac{3}{4}$

100°

80°

do, for example putting curly maple arms on a walnut chair, I mix them for aesthetic, not structural, reasons.

For this particular example, I chose to use curly maple throughout.

## Steam Bending

Because the slats have to be bent, I began by planing the slat stock to a $\frac{1}{4}$" thickness. I then sawed out the profiles on the band saw. Next, with a spokeshave and a rasp, I shaped a rounded bevel on the top edges of the middle of the slat.

My steamer is a deep-fat fryer my wife bought 20 years ago at a garage sale. I cut a round hole in the fryer's metal lid to accept one end of a 48" length of 4" diameter PVC. I fastened wire mesh across the bottom of the PVC to hold parts above the water during steaming. I also bought a cap for the top of the PVC to hold in the steam—although I found I get the best flow through the PVC by drilling a half dozen holes through the cap or by cocking the cap at an angle so that a bit of the top of the PVC pipe is exposed. Without this ventilation, the steam tends to escape around the lid of the deep-fat fryer, rather than traveling up through the PVC around the parts I want to steam.

The design of your steamer is limited only by your imagination. All that's required is a source of heat to boil water and an enclosure to hold the wood parts while the steam passes by them.

Because they're so thin, the slats need to spend only 30 minutes in the steamer. I then pull them out, place them in my bending jig, and squeeze them into shape in the bending forms which are held between the jaws of my bench vise. I have several extra benches in my shop, so I just leave the slats in the vise until the bends have set, but in the past, when I needed the vise for other uses, I locked the two parts of the slat-bending jig together with clamps or U-bolts and then removed them from the vise.

The bent parts should then be set aside for about a week so that the bends can set.

While the slats are curing in the bending forms, you can turn your attention to the chair's other parts. Like the slats, the rockers are sawn out from stock thicknessed to the correct dimension. Use a plane to true up the bottom edges of the rockers so that those surfaces present a gradual and consistent curve. The top edges are a little trickier to fair. I used a spokeshave and a rasp.

## Turning

The back posts of Shaker chairs require lathes with an unusually long distance between centers, often over 44". Twenty years ago, when I began making chairs, I didn't have the money to buy a good big lathe, so I bought a cheap small lathe and modified it to accept long stock. In

**TOP** My steamer is a garage-sale french fryer, into the lid of which I cut an opening large enough to accept a 4" PVC pipe. I hold the creaky assembly upright by fastening it to a chair with a loop of splint.

**BOTTOM** I sandwich the freshly steamed slats between the two parts of the slat bending form. In a week, they'll be ready to remove.

my case, the modification consisted of welding a second mounting foot to the end of the tubular lathe bed that would ordinarily have fit into the headstock. This allows me to move the tailstock anywhere I want, giving me a lathe with a theoretically infinite distance between centers. Although my technique for lengthening my lathe bed might not work for you, I've never yet seen a lathe that couldn't be lengthened—although some take more

head scratching than others.

Even experienced turners can struggle to turn the long, thin parts required by Shaker chairmaking. The front rungs and back posts in particular can be challenging to control because what you find is that if you push your tool against a long, thin piece of work that's spinning in your lathe, the work will flex away from the tool, resulting in chatter as the work vibrates against the tool. To reduce the tendency of the work to flex, I have three suggestions:

1. Choose a mid-range lathe speed. I use 1350 rpm. If you turn with excessive speed, there is a danger of the work coming apart in the lathe or breaking loose from its centers, and a 44" post blank cartwheeling from your lathe can wreak havoc on you, your shop and your peace of mind. Conversely, if the speed is too slow, my perception is that the work gives too easily under the pressure of the lathe tool. This is something I'm not enough of a scientist to explain, but my perception is informed by many years of experience.

2. Don't push the tool into the work. Lay the bevel on the work, and lift the handle until the edge engages the work. There will always be some pressure of tool against work, but I think it's helpful to avoid thinking of the spinning work/lathe tool interface as a point of resistance requiring force.

3. Use your off hand as a steady rest. I wrap a few turns of masking tape around my right hand (I'm left handed), and that protects my hand from friction burns when I use it to lightly support the back side of the spinning work.

I recommend that inexperienced chair makers begin by turning the short back and side rungs and then move onto the posts, saving the tricky back posts for last.

A post-and-rung chair is held together by fitting round rung tenons into round mortises cut into the posts. I use a $9/16$" Forstner bit which produces very consistent and accurate mortises. The tenons require a bit more skill to fashion accurately. I begin with a $1/2$" fingernail gouge and create a hollow in the tenon I'm about to form. When the least diameter of that hollow is $9/16$", I switch to a 1" butt chisel laid bevel-side-down on the rest. I then move that into the work and scrape the tenon to size until the diameter along its entire length equals its least diameter. I then cut a $1/16$" taper on the end of the tenon to enable it to better slide into its mortise.

Notice that the rungs taper from a greatest diameter of about $7/8$" to a least diameter of about $5/8$" at the shoulder next to each tenon.

The back posts also taper, from a diameter of about $1 3/8$" just above the seat rungs to a diameter of about $1 1/8$" just below the shoulder at the base of the finial. The cove

at the base of the finial, which I form with a $^1/2$" fingernail gouge, has a least diameter of about $^1/2$".

After I've turned a run of chair parts, I re-center each and lathe sand them through a succession of grits: 100, 150, 220.

## Marking the Posts

My lathe has an indexing head which simplifies the process of accurately marking rung mortises, but it is possible to produce usable markings without the use of a lathe with an indexing head. I'll describe both methods.

An indexing head is a disk centered on the lathe's axis of rotation which has holes bored at regular intervals near the disk's circumference. The indexing head on my lathe has 36 equally spaced holes, which means I can divide any object turned on my lathe into 36 equal segments, each of which is 10 degrees from the next. My lathe also has a spring-loaded pin on the headstock which allows me to lock the lathe's indexing head (and its rotation) at each of those 36 stops.

The centerlines of the front rungs on this particular rocking chair are 80 degrees from the centerlines of the side rungs. To mark the front posts, I select a location for the center of the front-rung mortises and lock the lathe's rotation with the spring-loaded pin so that the centerline is facing me. I then slide my marking jig along my lathe bed so that its pencil marks a line along the length of the front post. I then click off eight stops (80 degrees) on my indexing head, lock the indexing head, and with my marking jig, make a second line marking the center of the side-rung mortises.

I then lay my front-post story stick along the post and mark rung centers along each of the two lines I made using my marking jig; one set of marks locating front rung mortises, the other marking side rung mortises.

I use the same procedure to mark the back posts with one exception: The centerline of the side rungs is 100 degrees from the centerline of the back rungs, which means counting off ten stops on the indexing head. I then mark rung-mortise locations (and slat mortise locations) along the two lines on the back posts.

If you don't have an indexing head on your lathe, you can achieve a very similar result on your bench top.

Rip a wide, flat carpenter's pencil in half along its length so that the lead (graphite) is exposed. Snug up a pair of front posts on your bench side to side with their ends aligned. Then run a ripped half of the carpenter's pencil along the snugged up posts, lead down, with its length perpendicular to the lengths of the posts. In this manner, you'll create a line on each post that is parallel to the post's centerline. Then rotate the posts so that these centerlines are facing one another, and once again snug up the posts and draw lines along their lengths using the ripped carpenter's pencil. These second lines will be 90 degrees from the first pair of lines.

Do the same with the back posts.

In each case, you'll have lines 10 degrees from ideal placements, ten degrees too far on the front posts and ten degrees not far enough on the back posts. Fortunately, those errors don't matter because the side-rung-mortise jig will create accurate placements on the circumferences of the posts. All you need at this point are approximations along which you can mark the rung mortises.

The front and back rung mortises are drilled next using the front-rung-mortise jig (FRMJ) This jig should be set up so that its fence is a distance from the lead point

on your Forstner bit that is half the diameter of the post. So if your posts are the ideal diameter of 1³/₈", you will set the fence ¹¹/₁₆" from the lead point. Also, you should set the depth stop on your drill press so that you're drilling mortises ¹⁵/₁₆" deep. This will accept ⁷/₈" long tenon and allow a bit of extra length as a glue reservoir.

The front ladder can be assembled at this time. Be sure to check it for square before setting it aside to dry.

## Chopping Slat Mortises

After a week in the bending forms, you can remove the slats and begin chopping slat mortises in the back posts.

I chop slat mortises by hand, using a mortise chisel that is ground to a width a bit less than the ¹/₄" thickness of the slats. I begin by clamping the steam-bent post to my bench with the locations of the slat mortises up.

Before you cut any slat mortises, study the photos accompanying this chapter carefully. There are two important considerations. First, the front (relative to the finished chair) of the slat mortise is placed on the centerline of the back-rung mortises. This is the centerline you made when you were marking the rung mortises. Second, the slat mortises have to enter the post at an angle relative to the centerlines of the back rungs.

I place a back rung upright in the bottom back-rung mortise as a reference rung when I'm chopping slat mortises. The angle at which I chop those mortises must align the slat so that a line connecting its two ends is parallel to the centerline of the back reference rung.

With a marking knife, I define the front and back of each slat mortise. I then begin chopping them out with my mortise chisel, making frequent checks of my angle by placing a rung in the half-finished mortise and sighting from the bottom of the post.

Notice that the drawing indicates a different tenon length for different slats. The tenon length simply indicates the amount of slat that penetrates the post. There is no shoulder.

Once the slat mortises have been chopped, the back ladder can be assembled. Begin by clamping one post, mortise-side up, to your bench top. Then glue the tenons on each of the slats and back rungs and install those tenons in their mortises on the clamped post. Then start the tenons into their mortises on the other post.

This will be impossible.

At least that's what you'll think at first.

There are simply too many parts to get started all at once, but if you take your time, working from one end of the post to the other, starting each tenon as you go, eventually you will get them all simultaneously started. Then remove the assembly from your bench and, standing behind the partially assembled back ladder, lay a clamp across the front of the ladder. Then, starting at the bot-

**TOP** When all the posts have been turned, you can drill the front rung mortises and the back rung mortises using the front-rung-mortise jig (FRMJ) shown here. The post is attached to a carriage which slides underneath the Fortsner bit through the use of two wood screws which pass through a tail piece on the carriage and then penetrate into the end grain of the post.

**BOTTOM** The slat mortises should be chopped at an angle that allows the two ends of the slat to align with the two ends of the reference rung I have in the bottom of the post. I periodically check this alignment by sighting down the length of the post from the top.

tom of the ladder, begin drawing the two posts together, a bit at a time, working your way up and down the ladder with the clamp. Often, the slats will get stuck in their mortises. I coax them into place by squeezing together the middle of the slat and the bar on the clamp (when the posts are under the pressure of the clamp). This causes the ends of the slat to pop further into their mortises.

Carefully wash away any glue squeeze-out. I find a toothbrush and a bit of water is ideal for getting glue out of the intersections of rungs and post. Give the ladder a check for square by standing the ladder and a framing square together on your bench. The posts will splay just a bit as they rise from the bench. What you want is an equal amount of splay on each side.

Then set the ladder aside to dry.

## Assembling the Chair

The side-rung-mortise jig (SRMJ) simplifies the process of drilling accurate side rung mortises. It is designed so that, in one position, it will drill the mortises on the front ladder: mortises with centerlines 80 degrees from the centerlines of the mortises for the front rungs. Then, by turning the jig around 180 degrees on your drill press table, you can drill the supplementary angles for the mortises on the back ladder: mortises with centerlines 100 degrees from the centerlines of the mortises for the back rungs.

As you did with the FRMJ, the SRMJ should be set so that its fence, in both the front ladder and the back ladder positions, is a distance from the lead point of the Forstner bit that is half the diameter of the post. And here too, the drill press depth stop should be set to drill a $15/16$" deep mortise.

Study the photos in *Quick and Easy Jigs and Fixtures* detailing the use of this jig before you actually drill any mortises. I would also recommend that you turn a bit of scrap to the right diameter and, holding that scrap against the fence, cut a couple of mortises in that scrap to make sure you have the jig set up the way you want it.

You'll notice that, even when the jig is set up correctly, the lead point on the Forstner bit may not hit your marks dead center. That's not necessarily because you have the jig set up incorrectly—although it may be. Instead, the error is most likely a marking error.

**FACING PAGE TOP** The side rung mortises are drilled using the side-rung-mortise jig (SRMJ) shown here. The jig allows you to accurately bore the 100 degree angles in the back ladder and—by rotating the SRMJ 180 degrees on the drill press table—the 80 degree angles for the side rungs in the front ladder.

It's very difficult to get pencil lines that are dead on the right location around the outside diameter of the post. A properly set up jig, however, will find the exact locations.

When the mortises have been drilled in both the front and back ladders, you're ready to assemble the chair. Lay the back ladder front-side-up on your bench. Apply glue to all the side rung tenons. Then start the tenons in the mortises in the back ladder. At this point, lay the front ladder on top of the protruding side rungs and start the tenons into their mortises. When all the tenons have been started, stand the chair upright on your bench. Then, with a pipe or bar clamp, press the tenons into their mortises.

At this point, you need to check the stance of the chair on a reliably flat surface. I use my ground-steel table saw top for this purpose. If the four feet of your chair don't all meet the flat surface at the same time, rack the chair until they do.

Then step back and sight the chair from the front. Sight the alignment of each front post against the back post behind it. They won't align perfectly because the back ladder splays a bit as it rises from the surface. What you want to see is the same amount of splay on the right and left sides of the chair. If you see error, try to correct it by racking the chair.

No chair will be absolutely dead-on perfect, so don't expect to see that. When you get as close to perfection as you can manage, wash off the squeeze-out. Then set the chair aside to dry.

## Installing the Rockers

Because the rockers on this particular chair have flats sawn into their upper edges where the posts and rockers intersect, rocker installation is much easier than it is when you're installing rockers with curved upper edges. In the case of this chair, simply cut notches $1^7/16$" deep and just barely wide enough to accept the rockers.

Although some makers use a table saw to cut rocker notches, I don't recommend that practice. Instead, I use a fine-toothed backsaw to define the widths of the notches. I then drill a $1/4$" diameter hole through and through at the base of each notch. This hole makes it easy to break out the waste. I finish by paring the notch to fit the rocker.

I use $1/4$" dowels to hold the rockers in place. Each of these dowels passes through the post and the rocker at about the midway point of the notch's depth.

## Weaving the Seat

You can find a discussion of seat weaving in several different books, including my book *Authentic Shaker Furniture* which includes drawings of the jigs mentioned in this chapter.

# Miniature Blanket Chest

MATERIAL: *walnut, poplar, brass*
LOCATION: *first floor, Centre Family Dwelling*

### Reproducing the Blanket Chest

Furniture reproductions are never exactly like the originals on which they're based. In some cases, that's because the skill and artistry of the reproducer don't measure up to the skill and artistry of the original craftsman. In other cases, it's because the reproducer consciously made the decision to vary from the original, substituting curly maple for cherry or machine-cut dovetails for hand-cut dovetails. In other cases, it's because the reproducer decided that the original could be improved on in some way.

The last is true of my version of this delightful little blanket chest.

The original was appealing in several ways: diminutive size, charming country-style details, solid joinery. But it also had some problems. Instead of the chest bottom's edges being let into grooves cut on the inside surfaces of the four sides of the case, the bottom of the original was simply nailed inside the case. When the solid-wood bottom underwent its inevitable shrinkage across its width, gaps appeared on either side, visible when you sight into the case from above. The material also seems too thick for this relatively dainty form. The material of the original was dressed to a chunky $7/8$". I opted for $5/8$" material throughout, and I set the edges of the bottom into grooves (the drawing shows the original $7/8$" material).

I think the original might have been an apprentice piece. The master in the shop would have discouraged the youngster from testing his skills on a full-sized piece with a full-sized appetite for material, directing that youngster instead to this little miniature. The too-heavy material could be a result of the apprentice's desire to quickly get to the cool part, the cutting-dovetails part. That would also explain the missing grooves. After cutting all the joinery and gluing up the case, my theoretical

**LEFT** Unlike the maker of the original chest, who employed only walnut heartwood as a primary wood, I incorporated sapwood into the cherry lid of my reproduction.

**FACING PAGE** Some past caretaker of this dainty chest decided, for reasons unknown, to stand it up on fir framing-stock blocks which are glued in place inside the chest's bracket feet. These blocks account for the chest's curious posture.

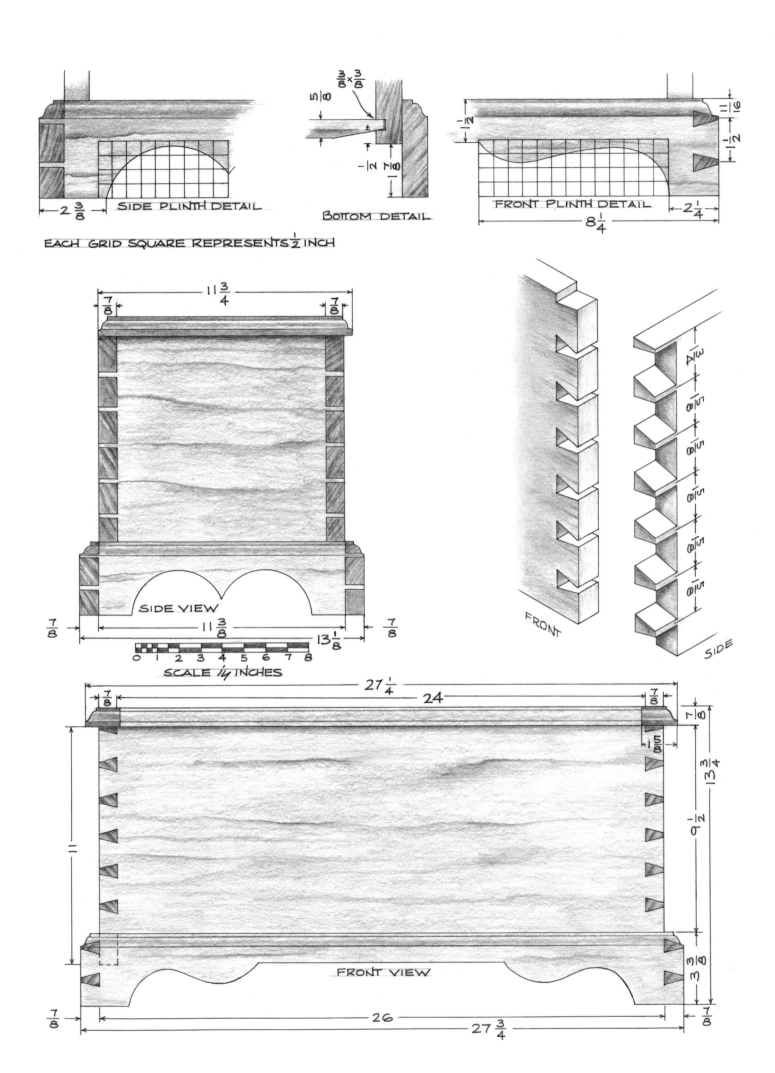

$\frac{3}{8} \times \frac{3}{8}$

$\frac{5}{8}$

$\frac{1}{2}$

$\frac{7}{8}$

$2\frac{3}{8}$

SIDE PLINTH DETAIL

BOTTOM DETAIL

$\frac{1}{2}$

$\frac{11}{16}$

$\frac{1}{2}$

FRONT PLINTH DETAIL

$2\frac{1}{4}$

$8\frac{1}{4}$

EACH GRID SQUARE REPRESENTS $\frac{1}{2}$ INCH

$\frac{7}{8}$

$11\frac{3}{4}$

$\frac{7}{8}$

$\frac{7}{8}$

SIDE VIEW

$11\frac{3}{8}$

$\frac{7}{8}$

$13\frac{1}{8}$

0 1 2 3 4 5 6 7 8

SCALE IN INCHES

FRONT

SIDE

$\frac{3}{4}$

$\frac{5}{8}$

$\frac{5}{8}$

$\frac{5}{8}$

$\frac{5}{8}$

$\frac{5}{8}$

$\frac{5}{8}$

$27\frac{1}{4}$

24

$\frac{7}{8}$

$\frac{7}{8}$

$\frac{7}{8}$

$\frac{1}{8}$ CUT

$13\frac{3}{4}$

11

$9\frac{1}{2}$

$3\frac{3}{8}$

FRONT VIEW

$\frac{7}{8}$

26

$\frac{7}{8}$

$27\frac{3}{4}$

**TOP LEFT** If possible, cut lengths from the same board for each piece of a panel you are going to glue up. This offers the best possible color and figure match.

**LEFT** After squaring lines across the end grain, I cut the sides of each tail freehand, without first marking those sides with a gauge. This gives me joinery that is certifiably hand cut, with each tail just a little different from the one beside it.

apprentice looked down into it, slapped himself on the forehead and said: "I forgot to cut the grooves."

At least that's my theory.

So why would I reproduce a piece that I think might have been the work of an apprentice?

Well, I like it.

## The Big Three-hearted Tree

Material selection and arrangement is always critical, but it is doubly so in the case of a very simple piece like this on which there isn't any carving or veneering to seduce the eye.

When I'm gluing up panels for such a piece, I begin by pulling boards with similar color and figure.

I then begin to layout the cuttings on the surfaces of those boards, making an effort to ensure each panel will be glued up of pieces taken from the same board. This means, for example, that the five pieces from which the lid is glued up were all taken from the same board. Three 25" sections of that board came together for the lid's main panel. The breadboard ends were then ripped from the offcut left behind. This approach is critical, I believe, because even though all the boards I might pull for a particular piece will have similar color and figure, the very best matches are those taken from the same board.

We woodworkers are often tempted to line up our

cuttings along the edges of our boards. That is, after all, the logical way to proceed. You joint one edge, set the table saw to the desired width, then rip off what you need. That's an efficient use of time and material, but it doesn't always result in the most visually pleasing arrangement of material. My method is to draw rectangles anywhere on the boards that have the kind of color, figure and absence of defects I'm trying to attain. Then I band saw the first long edge of the piece, joint that edge, and cut the other side on the table saw.

I consciously look for opportunities to employ material exhibiting a mix of heart and sapwood, particularly in the cases of walnut and cherry where the contrasts are so dramatic. However, the use of sapwood places on me the obligation to use that material in some kind of aesthetically coherent manner. In the case of this blanket chest, I decided I would use sapwood only on the lid and only in a very controlled context. Specifically, I would create two swaths of light-colored material running the full length of the lid, stopped and held visually in place by breadboard ends cut from heartwood.

To create these two swaths of light-colored material, I aligned the material so that the joints between boards would occur only in the sapwood where, I knew from long experience, they would disappear, leaving the arresting appearance of a board cut from a three-hearted tree.

The molded edges on the original chest are battered. I suspect they were not very cleanly cut in the first place, and they have been abused by a century and a half of life at Pleasant Hill and elsewhere. The result is that it was difficult to tell exactly how they were originally intended to look. The drawing represents my best guess about the original maker's intentions, but the molding I used for my reproduction is the profile cut by a stock router bit—a $5/32$" Roman ogee on a $1/4$" shank—a bit that cuts a profile that's reasonably close, but not exactly like what I think the original maker intended.

### Build a Box and a Half

This chest consists of two boxes: one with a top and bottom and one without the plinth. The front, back and sides of each box are assembled with dovetails.

After you've glued up the panels from which each of the primary box's elements will be cut, level and smooth the panels with your planer or a set of hand planes. Then joint one edge of each panel, rip it to width (leaving a little surplus width to remove when you joint away the saw marks). Then cut each panel to width.

Before you start cutting dovetails, plow the grooves on the inside surfaces of the chest's larger box in which the box's bottom will be housed. You don't need stopped grooves for this particular chest because the through

grooves that would otherwise show on the ends of the chest are concealed by the plinth.

Then begin cutting dovetails. I cut my dovetails by hand because that's the only way I know how, but I understand they can be cut just as easily with a jig and a router. Apply glue to all mating surfaces of the dovetails and assemble the larger box around the chest bottom (the edges of which you've already beveled so they will fit in the grooves you've plowed for those edges). Check the case for square by measuring the diagonals. If there is an error, correct that error by racking the longer diagonal until the two measurements are the same (within maybe $1/32$"). Then wash away all the glue squeeze-out on the inside and outside of the chest.

Once the glue has cured, at least eight hours, fix the chest to your bench and, with a plane, pare down the surplus length from the pins and tails of your joinery. Prior to cutting a set of dovetails, I set my marking gauge so there is at least $1/32$" of extra length on these elements. Then I can plane the surplus flush to remove the end-grain tear out that is part of every saw cross cut.

I believe this planing is the most difficult part of the joinery process because it takes a fair amount of force to power even a sharp, well-tuned plane through end grain. That means the case must be securely fastened to your bench. I use a pair of bar clamps to hold the bottom side of the chest to the bench top. I also use a pipe clamp to hold the top side of the chest against the racking this planing can induce.

This work can be done with a belt sander, but the results are never as true as the results you can get with a plane.

Next, assemble the four parts of the plinth (the half box) using dovetails here as well. I chose to cut the joinery before I shaped the molding because I wasn't sure how I would mark the dovetails on an edge that had already been shaped.

Check the fit against the case dry to ensure there are no gaps. Then run the stock past the bit on your router table to create the molded edge. Before you glue up the four parts of the plinth, dry assemble them one more time, and mark the corners as shown at the top of page 118. You can very quickly remove most of the waste on your band saw, but it's very important to stay well above the line when you do that cutting.

Then glue up the plinth while the glue is still wet and attach the plinth to the case using $1^1/4$" #8 drywall screws. (I probably could have gone with 1" screws because the two pieces I'm joining here have a total thickness of only $1^1/4$", but I wanted the holding power of the longer screws, so before I used them, I touched the tip of each to my grinding wheel to reduce the length to a bit more than $1^1/8$".)

**TOP LEFT** It's important to dry fit the case (without fully seating the dovetails) to make sure everything's going to come together well.

**LEFT** Because I cut the pins and tails a little long (this is explained in the text), I use cleats to apply clamping pressure behind these elements when I'm bringing a case together.

**BOTTOM LEFT** Check the fit of the plinth elements around the case before you glue them together. Notice that I haven't yet cut the molded edge on the top of each element.

**RIGHT** I used a ⁵⁄₃₂″ Roman ogee bit to cut the molded edge. I used the same bit with the same set-up to cut the molded edge around the assembled top. Before you glue up the plinth, mark and cut away on your band saw the surplus stock at each corner.

**BELOW** Use clamps (and protective clamping blocks) to bring the plinth together and—this is important—screw it to the case before the glue in the dovetails cures. (If you look closely, you can see the bevels around the field of the raised panel on the chest bottom. These bevels were cut freehand with a jack plane.)

The molded corners of the plinth will require a little fussy work with hand tools in that end section you roughed in with your band saw. I used a shoulder plane to extend the little fillet at the base of the molded edge all the way to the corner. I then formed the rest of the molded edge with a paring chisel and a carving gouge plus a little sandpaper.

I couldn't really tell how the original lid's breadboard ends are attached. What I can say is this: There's no evidence of a tongue-and-groove joint (the joinery I would have used). That is, there is no tongue visible on the front edge of the lid. It's conceivable, however, that the tongue and groove were stopped, but that's a level of joinery sophistication I found nowhere else on this piece. In fact, for the most part, the joinery on this chest is very simple and straightforward—very Shaker. My guess is that the ends are fastened in place with floating tenons, mortised into both the end grain of the lid's main panel and the side grain of the breadboard ends. I chose to use a 20th-century standby, the lowly dowel. I applied glue only to the three center dowels. My thinking is that might permit a bit more movement across the grain of the center panel.

All lids cup. It's a natural law with results as predictable as gravity. It doesn't matter how carefully the material is seasoned or whether you've finished both top and bottom surfaces. All lids cup, and I have dedicated a good part of my woodworking life to finding ways to interfere with the expression of this natural law. In most case work, you can fasten the sides of the top to the sides of the case with good results, but you can't do that with a lid like the one on this chest. So many years ago I began installing cleats on the undersides of unsupported lids, and they do work, but they must be wide enough to resist cupping, and for best results you have to cheat with your cleats. Before I install them, I plane a $1/16$" crown on the edge that will contact the underside of the lid. This gives me some leverage in my war on cupping. I may not use it all at once. If, for example, there isn't much cupping on the day I install the cleats, I may install them with either end just a bit above the surface of the lid. Then later, if I need to, I can draw them down.

But I should point out that these cleats are not on the original lid, which, also, is cupped.

## Hardware

M-o-v-e v-e-r-y s—l—o—w—l—y.

I spent more than eight hours installing hardware on this chest, and for me that's good time. There are parts of the furniture construction process during which it's possible to work briskly, but hardware installation isn't one of them. Take your time with this process because a little haste here can ruin an otherwise handsome project.

Begin with the hinges. In the finished piece, the back side of the lid is aligned with the back side of the case. This simplifies the hinge installation by allowing you to cut hinge mortises in the edge of the lid, rather than in the interior of the lid's lower surface.

First attach both hinges to the bottom surface of the lid. Then hold the lid in place and have someone else mark the locations on the top edge of the chest back. Then cut the mortises in that top edge.

Next attach the two lid stays. These nifty bits of hardware were not on the original, but I think it's a mistake to attach any lid without also attaching something to prevent the lid from accidentally flopping all the way back and maybe pulling out the hinge screws.

The hinges and lid stays are available almost anywhere. I picked mine up at my local home improvement center.

An escutcheon almost exactly like the one on the original can be found at a woodworking supplier, as can the lock. Lock-and-strike-plate alignment can be frustrating. There is little room for error, and if you do make a slight mistake or if there is a slight mistake in lock manufacture, you may find yourself muttering in the shop.

Start the lock installation by locating the lengthwise center of the chest front and marking it with a pencil. Then close the lid on the chest and mark the lid overhang on the underside of the lid. Make another mark on the underside of the lid that lines up with the center line.

Remove the screws from the two lid stays and the two hinges, and place the lid top-down on a protected surface. Draw a second line parallel to the overhang line that is $5/16$" toward the back of the lid. This line defines the middle of the chest front's $5/8$" thickness. Align the strike plate mortise so that the plate will be installed directly above the front-to-back and side-to-side middle of the chest's front. Cut the mortise and install the strike plate.

Next, in the top edge of the chest front, cut the shallow mortise for the plate at the top of the lock mechanism, and cut the deeper mortise within the shallow mortise for the lock mechanism itself. Then drill the small hole through which the key shaft will pass to enter the lock mechanism. I recommend a Forstner bit for this hole because it cuts so cleanly. Finally, with a paring chisel, cut the mortise through which the tooth on the key will pass when it enters the lock.

You're ready to install your escutcheon.

## Finishing

Unfortunately, finishing is all about sanding. Lots of sanding. Use a block to keep the surface level and start with 100-grit sandpaper if there are any surface irregularities on the chest. Sand as long as you can stand it with 100-grit paper on your block. Then do it all over again with 100-grit paper. Switch to 150-grit and sand everything all over again. Twice. Then switch to 220-grit sandpaper and sand twice. Then 320-grit and sand twice. (Recently, I've been experimenting with an additional grit, using 600-grit before the first coat and 600-grit after the first coat of finish.)

In a small shop like mine, without a dedicated finishing room, I think woodworkers are much better off with wipe-on finishes. I've used many different brands, and all performed well. In the case of this chest, I used a wipe-on polyurethane, and two coats built up enough surface to lay a foundation for my paste wax. I sanded with 400 grit wet/dry paper after the first coat of poly. I sanded with 600 grit wet/dry after the second coat. I then applied the wax.

# Bed with Slatted Headboard

MATERIAL: *cherry, rope*
LOCATION: *second floor, Meeting House*

The Pleasant Hill collection includes a number of beds, and I considered all of those that had solid Pleasant Hill provenance before settling on this one. I chose this one simply because I like it. It represents, I believe, a clear and consistent design vision manifested by a workmanlike execution. This is a bed which I would enjoy having in our home if it were more appropriately sized.

It is supported on four classically simple, Pleasant Hill turned feet that taper slightly toward the floor. The headboard sides of the footboard posts widen nicely toward the bed, leading the eye into the piece. The headboard itself, which has a Mission-style flavor, consists of nine narrow slats mortised into the headboard's top and bottom rails.

It is simple, functional, graceful and without any features that detract from the design clarity. It is, in other words, perfectly Shaker.

**LEFT** The slanted inside face of the post makes a nice transition between the bed and the footboard.

**FACING PAGE** Like the many chairs in the Pleasant Hill collection, the diminutive size of this bed speaks to the changes in human stature over the past century and a half.

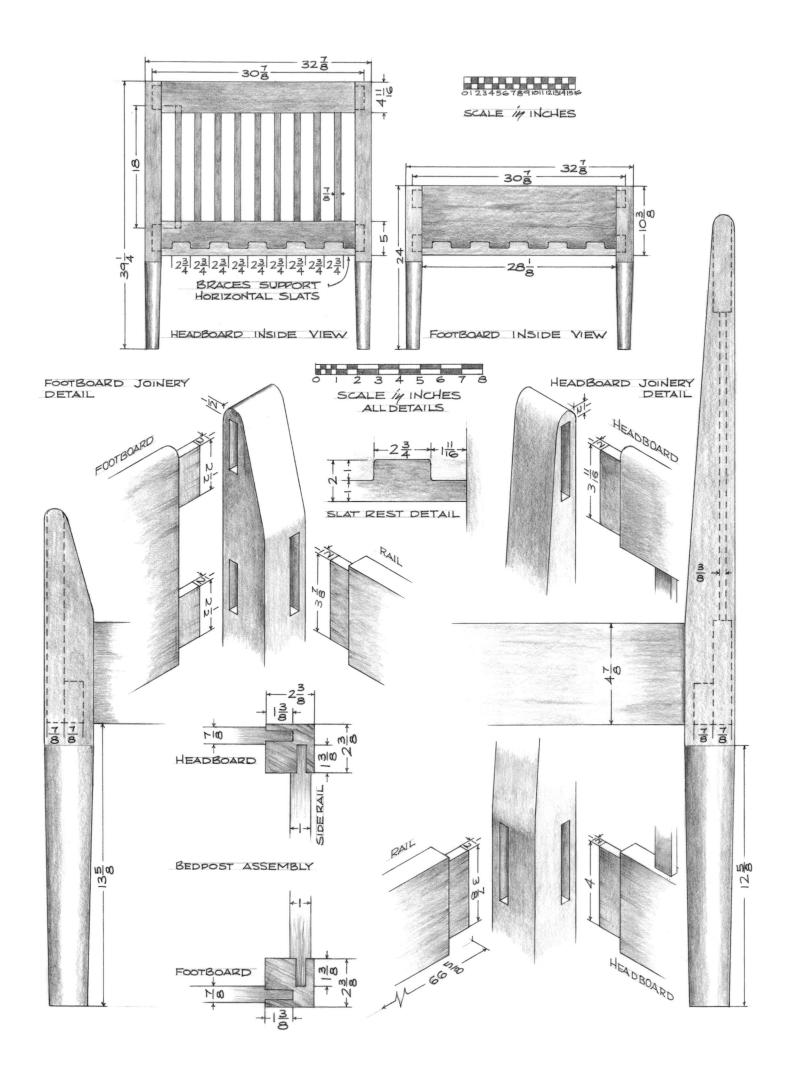

SCALE *in* INCHES

BRACES SUPPORT
HORIZONTAL SLATS

HEADBOARD INSIDE VIEW

FOOTBOARD INSIDE VIEW

FOOTBOARD JOINERY
DETAIL

SCALE *in* INCHES
ALL DETAILS

HEADBOARD JOINERY
DETAIL

FOOTBOARD

SLAT REST DETAIL

HEADBOARD

RAIL

HEADBOARD

SIDE RAIL

BEDPOST ASSEMBLY

FOOTBOARD

RAIL

HEADBOARD

**LEFT** This bag of dried flowers contained insect-repellent herbs. When it was explained to me what the bag contained, the curator added that the Shakers had planted carefully chosen flowers and herbs outside their windows to repel flying insects. The window could be opened without bugs entering the room.

**BELOW** The slatted headboard anticipates the look of some Mission-style pieces.

# Tripod Table

MATERIAL: *cherry, steel*
LOCATION: *third floor, Centre Family Dwelling*

**ABOVE** This is my interpretation of how the pedestal could be shaped.

**LEFT** This tripod-table form, which the Shakers adapted from sources in the World, is well suited to Shaker applications because it offers a maximum amount of table surface for a minimum expenditure of material.

Some of the Shaker tripod tables I've reproduced have underslung drawers hanging from runners that travel in rabbets cut into cleats which are screwed to the undersides of the tops (photo at left). Others, like this example, are simply tables.

The smallest Shaker tripod tables were probably used as candle stands, but this particular example is large enough so that its top could have served as a night stand with space for maybe a book and papers and a pair of glasses.

While I like the form and respect the workmanlike execution evident here, the pedestal on this table, like the pedestals on so many other Shaker tripod tables, is simply unlovely. Or maybe what I mean is that the pedestal is insufficiently lovely. When I look at this pedestal, I'm inevitably drawn to the amorphous lump above the cove. How much more attractive that pedestal would be if some of the material on the upper portion of that lump were turned away so that a long—and perhaps sensuous—line could be created that would run in one unbroken length all the way from the cove up to the bottom of the table.

But this table and others with similar pedestals have been widely reproduced so my opinion of the pedestal may be shared by very few observers of Shaker furniture.

Why then did I choose a table with a pedestal I don't really like? Well, I wanted to include a tripod table, and this one had the least unlovely pedestal I found at Pleasant Hill.

# Counter Chair

MATERIAL: *maple, oak, hickory, rush*
LOCATION: *second floor, Meetinghouse*

I changed my mind several times about whether or not I should add this chair to my list. On the one hand, it demonstrates, the insectile grace that I find so attractive in many Shaker chairs, particularly many of the side chairs in the Pleasant Hill collection, but on the other hand, it is something cobbled together, not something that represents a chairmaker's consistent vision.

I decided to keep it for two reasons. First, it is something cobbled together, and in the world of Shaker domestic life, that was often a virtue. When someone in the community needed a special-purpose chair, one with a seat raised to an unusual height, the Shaker craftsman who put this piece together decided he would add leg extensions to an existing chair rather than fashion a new one from scratch.

Typical Shaker frugality.

The second reason for keeping the chair is the fact that its apparent fragility gives me a chance to speak

**LEFT** This detail shows the extensions added to the chair legs. This is a construction I have seen in other Shaker chairs, although I've never taken one apart so I could learn exactly how it was done. My brother and I discussed this several times before we ended up with the result you see in the measured drawing. We could see only two realistic possibilities (although you could certainly think of other more exotic solutions to this problem.) Realistically, the extensions could have tenons reaching up into mortises drilled in the bottom of the chair posts or the bottoms of the posts could be reduced to tenons which would be fit into mortises in the extensions..

**FACING PAGE** The placement of this chair beside this secretary is appropriate not only because the unusual seat height of this chair complements the unusual height of the secretary's writing surface but also because each of the pieces in this pair is an adapted piece. The desk interior of the secretary was added—as an afterthought—to the top drawer of the unit's original chest of drawers, and the counter chair was raised to its current height by adding leg extensions, also as an afterthought.

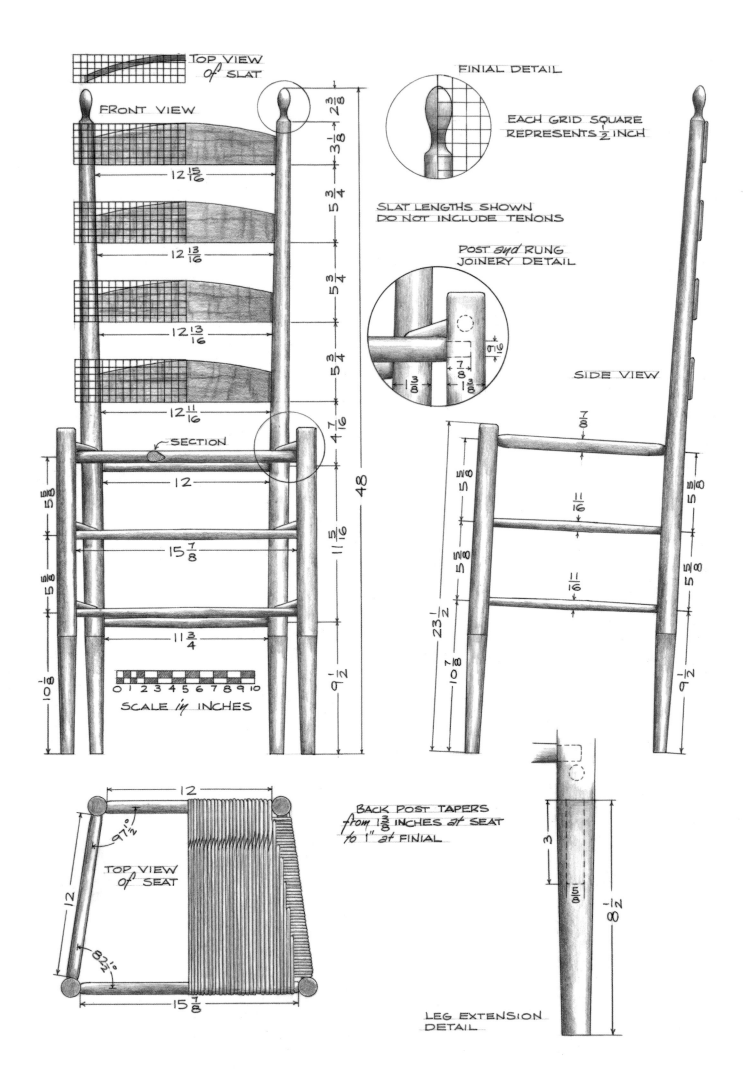

TOP VIEW *of* SLAT

FRONT VIEW

FINIAL DETAIL

EACH GRID SQUARE
REPRESENTS $\frac{1}{2}$ INCH

SLAT LENGTHS SHOWN
DO NOT INCLUDE TENONS

POST *and* RUNG
JOINERY DETAIL

SIDE VIEW

$12\frac{15}{16}$

$12\frac{13}{16}$

$12\frac{13}{16}$

$12\frac{11}{16}$

$2\frac{3}{8}$

$3\frac{3}{8}$

$5\frac{3}{4}$

$5\frac{3}{4}$

$5\frac{3}{4}$

$4\frac{7}{16}$

$48$

SECTION

$12$

$15\frac{7}{8}$

$11\frac{3}{4}$

$5\frac{5}{8}$

$5\frac{5}{8}$

$10\frac{1}{8}$

$11\frac{5}{16}$

$9\frac{1}{2}$

$\frac{9}{16}$

$\frac{7}{8}$

$\frac{3}{8}$

$\frac{3}{8}$

SCALE *in* INCHES

0 1 2 3 4 5 6 7 8 9 10

$\frac{7}{8}$

$5\frac{5}{8}$

$5\frac{5}{8}$

$\frac{11}{16}$

$\frac{11}{16}$

$5\frac{5}{8}$

$5\frac{5}{8}$

$23\frac{1}{2}$

$10\frac{7}{8}$

$9\frac{1}{2}$

TOP VIEW
*of* SEAT

$12$

$12$

$97\frac{1}{2}°$

$82\frac{1}{2}°$

$15\frac{7}{8}$

BACK POST TAPERS
*from* $1\frac{3}{8}$ INCHES *at* SEAT
*to* 1" *at* FINIAL

$3$

$8\frac{1}{2}$

$1\frac{5}{8}$

LEG EXTENSION
DETAIL

more thoroughly about a subject to which I have already alluded in this book: the 21st-century American corpus, or more precisely our corpora, which are considerably larger than the corpora of 19th-century Shakers and 19th-century Americans in general.

We are taller and wider and deeper (front to back) than any human beings in the 5,000,000 year history of our race. This is a situation that I suspect is a direct result of our nutrition.

We are not only well fed to an extent never before seen on this planet; some would argue that we are over-fed. This is a condition with enormous ramifications for chairmakers.

The Shaker chairs most Americans are familiar with are not the chairs, like this example, made in ones and twos and fours for the use of the Shakers in the many communities spread across the eastern half of the United States. Americans are most familiar with those chairs produced for sale to the World by the New Lebanon chairmaking operation under the direction of Brother Robert Wagan.

Wagan offered his chairs in several styles with seven sizes available in each style, with the #1 being the smallest—a child-sized chair—and the #7 being the largest—a chair intended for behemoths like Abe Lincoln.

The average American of the 19th century would have ordered a chair size from the middle of the Wagan spectrum, maybe a #3, a #4 or a #5.

Today, when I make chairs reproducing examples in that line, I never make anything smaller than a #5. In fact, many are #7s, and by far, the greatest number are #6s.

This delicate little confection probably would have been about right for a Shaker Eldress who stood 4' 7" and weighed about 80 pounds. In the average 21st-century American home, this chair would be used for display only.

(I include myself in the group of 21st-century Americans who should not sit in this chair. Regrettably, I am a much-too-robust 190 pounds.)

Joinery note: Kevin (my brother who did the illustrations for this book) and I could only guess at the joinery the Shaker craftsman used to attach the leg extensions to the legs. We considered dowels glued into mortises bored in the end grain at the bottoms of the legs and the tops of the extensions. We considered tenons turned onto the tops of the extensions, tenons which were then glued into mortises drilled into the end grain at the bottom of each post. But both of these options required a deep mortise to be drilled into the end grain at the bottom of each post.

On an assembled chair.

Very tricky work. I wouldn't want to attempt it.

**TOP** These finials are variants of the classic Pleasant Hill upside-down bowling pin.

**BOTTOM** Slat are not as comfortable as tape back chairs although—at least at Pleasant Hill—there are far more numerous.

That's why we eventually settled on tenons made from the foot of each post which were then glued into mortises drilled into the end grain at the top of each extension. This solution does require the craftsman to have had a tenon cutter of some kind to use on the legs of the chair, but I think that's a reasonable expectation.

The three-inch length of the tenon shown in the drawing is simply a guess.

# Side Table

MATERIAL: *cherry*
LOCATION: *basement dining room, Centre Family Dwelling*

After I assembled my first list of potential pieces, I asked Larrie Curry, the Pleasant Hill museum director, if there was anything that I hadn't included that she would like to include. She picked this sprightly little side table with legs tapering toward the floor in two directions.

**LEFT**  Shaker furniture, like the country furniture from which it arose, is not a furniture "period" like Queen Anne, Chippendale or Federal. Instead it is a genre that exists alongside the high-style work of each high-style furniture period. For example, the tripod table (page 125) borrows heavily from the Queen Anne period and the blanket chest on bracket feet (page 152) borrows heavily from the Chippendale period. Likewise, this dainty little specimen borrows heavily from the Hepplewhite period, named for the English designer George Hepplewhite.

**ABOVE**  Like many other Pleasant Hill tables, this example has no rail above the drawer front. The bottom of the tabletop serves as the kicker strip. (The kicker strip is a length of secondary wood the same thickness as the rail above the drawer. It extends out over the drawer on either side to keep the drawer properly aligned as it extends. Without the kicker strip the drawer front would lurch downward when the drawer is opened.)

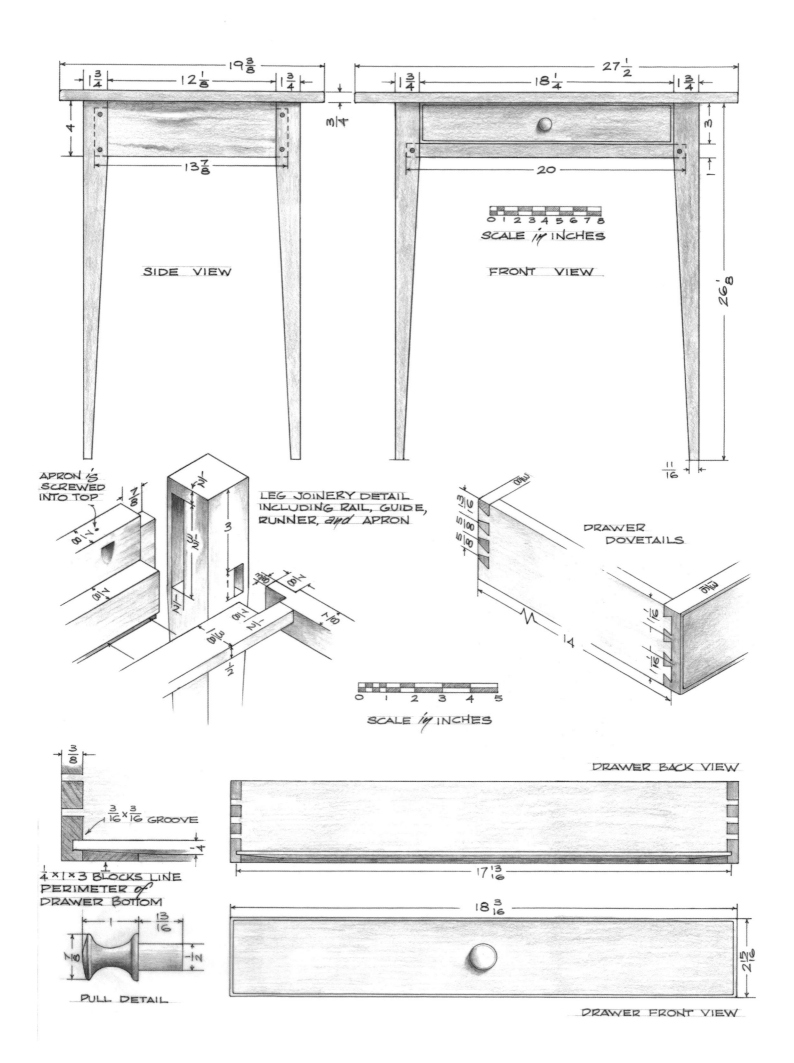

SIDE VIEW

FRONT VIEW

SCALE in INCHES

LEG JOINERY DETAIL
INCLUDING RAIL, GUIDE,
RUNNER, and APRON

APRON is
SCREWED
INTO TOP

DRAWER
DOVETAILS

SCALE in INCHES

DRAWER BACK VIEW

$\frac{3}{16} \times \frac{3}{16}$ GROOVE

$\frac{1}{4} \times 1 \times 3$ BLOCKS LINE
PERIMETER of
DRAWER BOTTOM

PULL DETAIL

DRAWER FRONT VIEW

The legs on this table have an elegant taper that is cut only on the inside faces of each leg. This gives the table a solid look but still lets it retain great poise. If the legs were tapered on the outside faces, it would appear top heavy.

# Red Cupboard

MATERIAL: *poplar*

LOCATION: *first floor, Centre Family Dwelling*

Although we don't know who made it, we do know when this cupboard was made.

Well, we think we do.

The following inscription appears on the back of the third interior shelf: "Began Dec. 1856. Finished Jan 1857."

In addition, there is a name on the inside of one of the doors: "Jane M."

Like most of the utilitarian furniture at Pleasant Hill, this jumbo cupboard is made from poplar, in this case dyed or stained red.

It features at each of the front corners a large quirked bead done in the return manner, which means that the bead was essentially cut twice. One time it was cut with the side bead molding plane positioned on the front of the stile. The second time the plane was positioned on the edge of the stile. This results in a bead that appears to stand proud from the corner.

**ABOVE** On the inside surface of the open door, you can see the greenish hue characteristic of poplar.

**LEFT** This detail shows the double-quirked or "return" bead.

**FACING PAGE** This massive piece features the extra wide stiles seen in many Shaker cupboards. The cupboard is rescued from clumsiness by its well shaped feet.

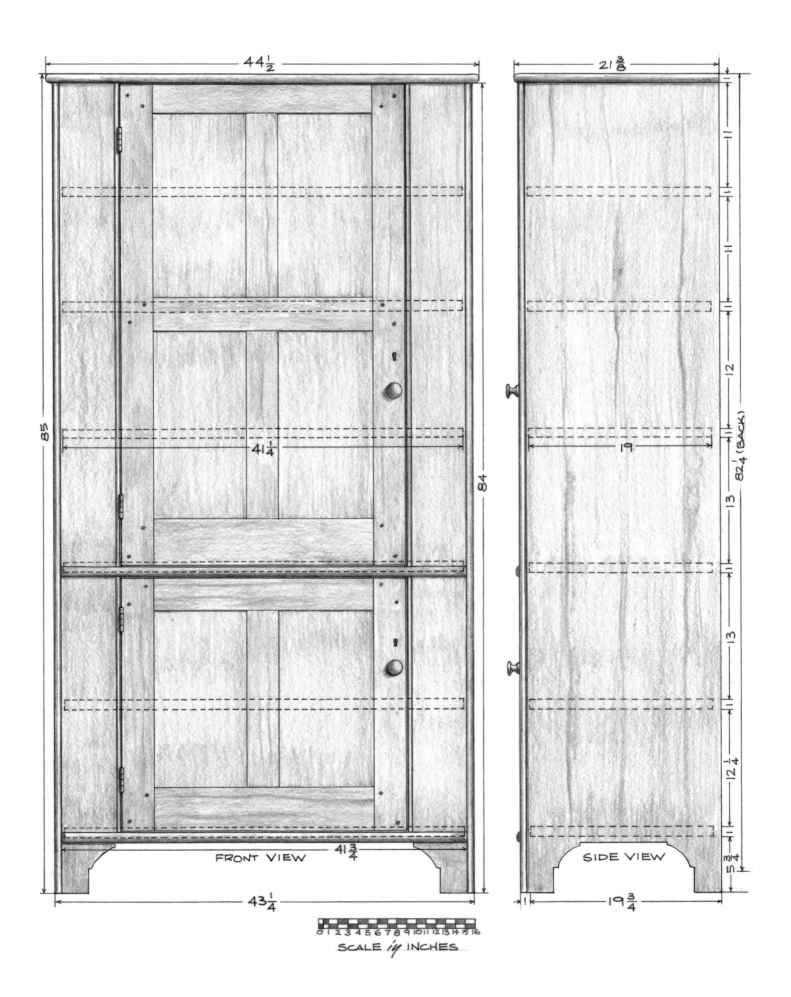

44½

21⅜

85

84

41¼

41¾

43¼

1

1

1

1

1

1

1

1

1

1

12

13

13

12¼

5¾

82¼ (BACK)

19

19¾

FRONT VIEW

SIDE VIEW

0 1 2 3 4 5 6 7 8 9 10 11 12 13 14 15 16

SCALE in INCHES

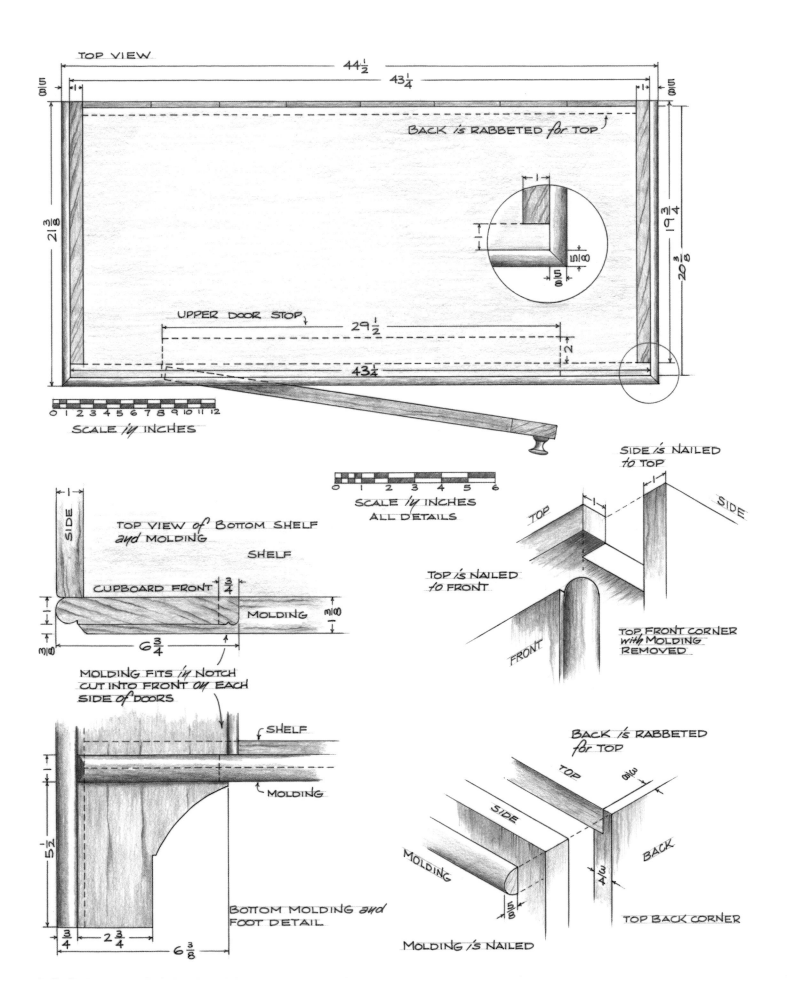

TOP VIEW

44 ½

43 ¾

BACK *is* RABBETED *for* TOP

21 ⅜

19 ¾

20 ⅜

1

1

⅝

⅝

UPPER DOOR STOP

29 ½

2

43 ¼

0 1 2 3 4 5 6 7 8 9 10 11 12

SCALE *in* INCHES

0 1 2 3 4 5 6

SCALE *in* INCHES
ALL DETAILS

SIDE

TOP VIEW *of* BOTTOM SHELF *and* MOLDING

SHELF

CUPBOARD FRONT

¾

MOLDING

³⁄₈

1

⅜

6 ¾

MOLDING FITS *in* NOTCH CUT INTO FRONT *on* EACH SIDE *of* DOORS

SHELF

1

MOLDING

5 ½

¾

2 ¾

6 ⅜

BOTTOM MOLDING *and* FOOT DETAIL

SIDE *is* NAILED *to* TOP

TOP

1

SIDE

TOP *is* NAILED *to* FRONT

FRONT

TOP, FRONT CORNER *with* MOLDING REMOVED

BACK *is* RABBETED *for* TOP

TOP

SIDE

⅜

BACK

MOLDING

⅝

¾

TOP BACK CORNER

MOLDING *is* NAILED

# Two-Drawer Blanket Chest

MATERIAL: *cherry, poplar*
LOCATION: *second floor, Meetinghouse*

This is one of three very similar blanket chests in the Pleasant Hill collection. All are housed in rooms on the second floor of the Meeting House, which made it easy to compare and contrast them.

Each one is built on a low base, consisting of four stubby legs into which the apron components are mortised. The legs terminate in classically simple Pleasant Hill turned feet. The hinged lids are made of solid wood with narrow breadboard ends. The interior of each chest includes a small till.

Each chest also displays the same curious feature in the dovetail joinery of the large upper case. Specifically, the dovetails on the back of the case are set into half-blind dovetail sockets chopped out of the case sides.

This is a characteristic I've seen elsewhere both inside and outside the world of Shaker furniture, with only a few exceptions, it is one I saw consistently in Pleasant Hill blanket chests.

Since there are three nearly identical chests of the same apparent vintage, of the same level of craftsmanship, each exhibiting the same joinery characteristic, it seems likely they are the work of the same hand or at least of the same shop under the direction of the same hand.

Also, there is another, apparently much older chest in the Centre Family Dwelling with the same style of dovetailing. Larrie Curry, the Pleasant Hill museum director, believes this piece might have been transported to Pleasant Hill, rather than made there, so it's possible that the three nearly identical Meeting House chests were inspired by the apparently older example in the Centre Family Dwelling.

Note: Each drawer front is embellished with a $3/16$" bead cut into the outer surface, probably with a scratch stock.

The pair of drawers under the main compartment of this chest not only makes the piece more interesting visually; it also makes the piece more useful.

**ABOVE** This is the classic Pleasant Hill turned foot given a dainty flavor by removing a little extra thickness just above the floor.

**RIGHT** The till and the two bottom drawers make this a very versatile piece of storage furniture.

# Kitchen Work Table

MATERIAL: *cherry*
LOCATION: *kitchen, Centre Family Dwelling*

My attitudes about furniture are subject to change.

When I first saw this colossal kitchen work table in the first hour of my first visit to Pleasant Hill, it confirmed the secret dislike I'd harbored for some of the Pleasant Hill furniture I'd seen in books and magazines. After a lifetime of studying and reproducing the much lighter constructions made in the Eastern Shaker communities, my prejudices were cast in concrete. Shaker work is light, my prejudices said. That is one of its fundamental virtues. Any work that isn't light isn't truly Shaker.

And this table isn't light. It's a behemoth, a brontosaurus thundering through a Shaker tradition populated with egrets and herons.

But somehow, over the last two years, this thick-necked stevedore has won me over with its honest, elephantine charm. Yes, it does demonstrate the thickness, the solidity, the stiffness that have kept Western Shaker furniture on the back porch, insistently knocking on the door, demanding to be invited inside to join the party, but, just maybe, it's time we opened the door.

**LEFT** Notice the splines used to align the boards on the tabletop.

**FACING PAGE** Although it lacks the complexity and ingenious design of other large pieces of Pleasant Hill furniture, by virtue of its size and its simple aesthetic coherence, I believe this table deserves to be seen as an important piece of Pleasant Hill furniture.

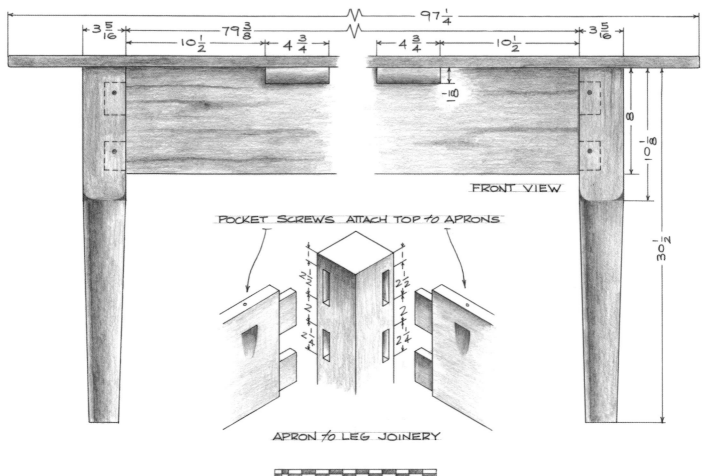

FRONT VIEW

POCKET SCREWS ATTACH TOP to APRONS

APRON to LEG JOINERY

0 1 2 3 4 5 6 7 8 9 10 11 12

SCALE 1/4 INCHES

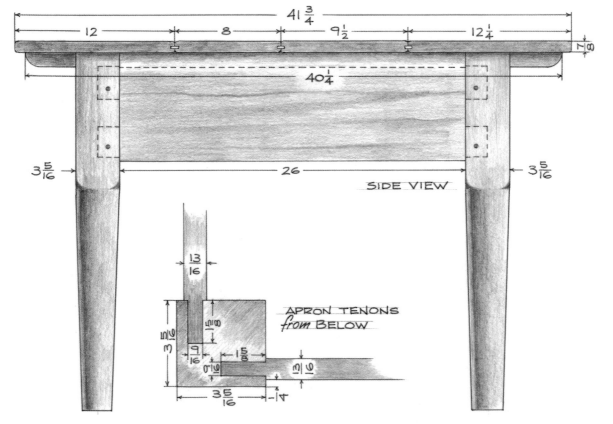

SIDE VIEW

APRON TENONS *from* BELOW

The heavy leg exhibits the minimal transition between square upper
section and turned lower section typical of much Pleasant Hill Furniture.

# Blanket Chest

MATERIAL: *cherry*

LOCATION: *third floor, Centre Family Dwelling*

At its best, a piece of Shaker furniture offers the viewer a coherent integrity of design. By that, I mean that all of the elements in its construction—the materials, the basic forms, the elaborations of those forms—all come together into something that makes sense in terms of function and visual presence.

The bed on page 120 is one such piece. So too is this simple chest. Except for a spare molded edge around the lid, another at the top of the plinth and the plainest possible bandsawn shape of the bracket feet, this piece is bereft of ornamentation. The front and the lid are nothing more than unbroken expanses of honest cherry.

**BELOW** Like the exterior, the interior of the chest is clean and uncluttered.

**LEFT** This carefully designed and crafted piece is one of the largest blanket chests in the Pleasant Hill collection.

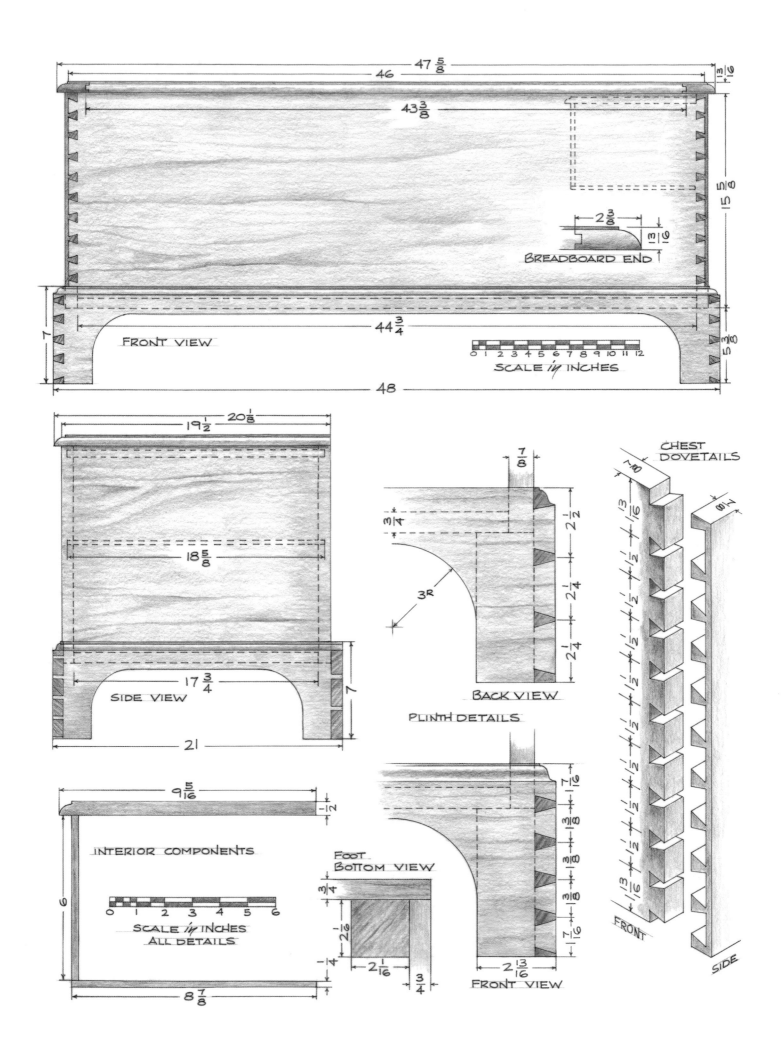

47 5/8

46

43 3/8

13/16

2 3/8

13/16

BREADBOARD END

15 5/8

7

44 3/4

FRONT VIEW

0 1 2 3 4 5 6 7 8 9 10 11 12

SCALE in INCHES

5 3/8

48

20 1/8

19 1/2

18 5/8

17 3/4

SIDE VIEW

7

21

7/8

3/4

2 1/2

3R

2 1/4

2 1/4

BACK VIEW

PLINTH DETAILS

CHEST DOVETAILS

1/4 0

13/16

1/2

1/2

1/2

1/2

1/2

1/2

1/2

1/2

1/2

1/2

13/16

1/4 8

FRONT

SIDE

9 5/16

1/2

INTERIOR COMPONENTS

FOOT
BOTTOM VIEW

3/4

6

0 1 2 3 4 5 6

SCALE in INCHES
ALL DETAILS

2 1/6

1/4

2 1/16

3/4

7/16

3 1/8

3 1/8

3 1/8

3 1/8

7/16

2 13/16

FRONT VIEW

8 7/8

**ABOVE** The breadboard ends of the lid are held in place via a tongue-and-groove joint which is visible at the front and back of each breadboard end.

**LEFT** The dovetail joinery on this chest is exceptional. Note the clean, consistent work at the corner of the chest and the plinth.

# The Restored Shaker Community at Pleasant Hill

In 1922, James L. Isenberg, a Harrodsburg businessman who had worked to acquire and reconstruct Old Fort Harrod before presenting it to the Commonwealth of Kentucky, purchased the Pleasant Hill Trustee's Office, thinking to repeat his Fort Harrod success at Pleasant Hill. His partner in this endeavor was C. B. Sullivan, who later took control of the properties with the idea of starting a Depression-era Arts and Crafts movement built on Ann Lee's most famous motto: "Put your hands to work and your heart to God." In the process, he restored the Trustee's Office, installing a Shaker museum there, and this marked the first important step on the long road toward the restoration we see today.

In the next few decades, several interested individuals and organizations tested the water. All expressed the desire to do something about preserving a place that was widely seen as a significant part of Kentucky history. However, despite their good intentions, none of those efforts managed to accomplish any more than Sullivan had.

The next important step was taken by a group headed by Earl D. Wallace, a Lexington businessman with the requisite skills and connections to get a project like this off the ground, and in August of 1961, largely as a result of Wallace's efforts, a charter was issued by the secretary-of-state's office, establishing Shakertown at Pleasant Hill as a nonprofit organization.

Those involved in the planned Shakertown restoration spent the next few years trying to raise the enormous amount of money the restoration would require. Ultimately, the funds were acquired through loans authorized by the Area Redevelopment Administration, which was authorized by Congress to lend funds to organizations which promised to provide long-term employment in under-employed areas.

Then, in 1965, two things happened which signaled the first major steps in the Pleasant Hill restoration. First, the Baptist congregation which had been holding its services in the Meeting House was moved to a new church just beyond the Pleasant Hill property. Second, U.S. 68, which had run right through the Pleasant Hill community, was rerouted south of the village.

Finally, in 1967, the first phase of the restoration began.

**RIGHT** Finished in 1834 under the direction of Pleasant Hill's architectural prodigy Micajah Burnett, the Centre Family Dwelling was built of Kentucky limestone quarried on Pleasant Hill property. Today, it houses a number of rooms furnished as they might have been during the heyday of the Shaker era.

Visitors to the building are greeted at the door by costumed interpreters who lead the visitors from room to room, explaining the many furnishings on display there.

Most of those furnishings are of Pleasant Hill origin. Others are objects from Eastern communities gathered by Burwell Marshall. (This view shows the building from the Meeting House, which is directly opposite, across the turnpike.)

**ABOVE** The requisite separate staircases, one for Brethren and one for Sisters, give the interiors of the buildings an arresting visual balance and rhythm.

**RIGHT** This view of the western façade of the Centre Family Dwelling indicates the enormity of this structure, including the ell at the rear of the building's primary mass. The first floor of the Centre Family Dwelling alone occupies more than 6000 square feet. Note the number of windows, all of which required large sashes (and frames), work that would have been accomplished in one of the community's woodshops.

**LEFT** The meeting room on the second floor of the Centre Family Dwelling had to be large enough to accommodate the Dwelling's many occupants.

**BELOW** The Trustee's Office is one of several architectural masterpieces attributed to Micajah Burnett.

**RIGHT** No visit to Pleasant Hill is complete without a stop in the Trustee's Office to marvel at the twin circular stairways which rise three stories in parallel magnificence.

**LEFT** The waiting areas for the Pleasant Hill dining room are located in the two semicircular sections of floor under the circular stairways.

**ABOVE** Fairly early in the architectural history of Pleasant Hill, the community's primary architect, presumably Micajah Burnett, began to introduce curvilinear forms into the village's buildings. The most glorious example of this was, of course, the circular stairway in the Trustee's Office, but this concept found expression in other contexts as well. This view of the entrance doors to the Trustee's Office shows the wide, fan-shaped window that surmounts the doors.

**RIGHT** Although the exterior of the Centre Family Dwelling is severely rectilinear, the interior is softened through the use of a number of curved elements, like this arched doorway.

**ABOVE** A gravel road now bisects the community on the route once occupied by the Lexington to Harrodsburg turnpike. The Centre Family Dwelling is on the left, the Meeting House on the right.

**FACING PAGE TOP** When he set out to create the Meeting House, the primary design problem confronting Micajah Burnett was how to provide an enormous open room in which the entire population of Pleasant Hill might come together in a worship service that involved a great deal of sometimes frenzied physical activity—all without colliding with any structural members required to support the building's upper story and roof. At the same time, the structure had to be sturdy enough to absorb the impact of hundreds of shaking Shakers.

Today, an architect would simply specify a steel framework for the building's second story. This option, however, was not available to Burnett, so he devised a system of trusses and beams to meet the needs of his religious community. Some of these structural members can be seen in the building's attic.

**FACING PAGE BOTTOM** The "Millennial Laws" dictated separate entrances for Brethren and Sisters, like these seen here on the Northern façade of the East Family Dwelling.

**ABOVE** The stone fences which border many Pleasant Hill fields served both to restrain livestock and as a repository for stone gleaned from fields.

**RIGHT** This headstone marks the final resting place of Francis Pennebaker, one of the last of the Pleasant Hill Shakers. (On page 29, Pennebaker is pictured with several sisters.)

# Final Thoughts

I often wonder what the 19th-century Shakers whose work I so admire would think about my admiration. Like many contemporary devotees of Shaker work, I have profound respect for what this relatively small group of 19th-century Americans accomplished in the material world. But that respect does not extend to what they accomplished in the spiritual world. In fact, the spiritual world the Shakers constructed seems to me to have been a little strange, a little eccentric and in their insistence on celibacy and the destruction of the nuclear family, contrary to what I must confess I see as the natural order.

The miracles the Pleasant Hill Shakers wrought in the Kentucky wilderness—particularly those under the direction of Micajah Burnett, the architect of its most magnificent buildings—leave me breathless. I struggle to comprehend the magnitude of the human effort involved in building something as imposing as the Centre Family Dwelling, without, we must not forget, the assistance of power equipment. And that was just one of many, many structures the Pleasant Hill Shakers designed, built, and furnished—all within a brief window of time.

That accomplishment is beyond my power to reckon, but I can acknowledge it. It is real, and it is, I believe, good. It represents an honest use of tools, materials and effort to meet a real human need for shelter. It stands as a towering monument to the human need to create.

But I can't say the same about a spirituality that ripped apart families in 19th-century America, a spirituality that separated wives from husbands and children from parents.

Instead, when I contemplate Shaker furniture making, I practice a kind of intellectual disconnect. I admire the accomplishments of the Shakers in the material world while consciously shutting out the spirituality that inspired those accomplishments.

The problem, of course, with such a view is that their accomplishments in the material world would have been impossible without their accomplishments in the spiritual world because it is only in the context of a larger-than-self purpose that the Shakers came willingly together to expend so much effort. The erection of the Centre Family Dwelling required an enormous sublimation of self, but it is also, paradoxically a profound expression of the human ego.

# bibliography

## Books

Allen, Douglas R.; Grant, Jerry V.. *Shaker Furniture Makers.* Hanover NH: University Press of New England, 1989.

Boice, Martha; Covington, Dale; Spence, Richard. *Maps of the Shaker West.* Dayton OH: Knot Garden Press, 1997.

Burks, Jean; Reiman, Tim. *The Complete Book of Shaker Furniture.* New York: Harry N. Abrams, 1993.

Clark, Thomas D.; Ham, F. Gerald. *Pleasant Hill and its Shakers.* Shakertown at Pleasant Hill: Pleasant Hill Press, 1968.

Giles, Janice Holt. *The Believers.* (a novel) Lexington KY: The University Press of Kentucky, 1957.

Kassay, John. *The Book of Shaker Furntiture.* Amherst MA: The University of Massachusetts Press, 1980.

Kirk, John T.. *The Shaker World.* New York: Harry N. Abrams, 1997.

Lancaster, Clay. *Pleasant Hill: Shaker Canaan in Kentucky.* Salvia KY: Warwick Publications, 2001.

Larkin, David; Sprigg, June. *Shaker Life, Work and Art.* Boston: Houghton Mifflin Co., 1987.

Muller, Charles R.; Rieman, Timothy D.. *The Shaker Chair.* Amherst MA: The University of Massachusetts Press, 1992.

Neal, Julia. *The Kentucky Shakers.* Lexington KY: The University Press of Kentucky, 1982.

Sack, Albert. *The New Fine Points of Furniture: Early American.* New York: Crown Publishers, Inc., 1993.

Thomas, James C.; Thomas, Samuel W.. *The Simple Spirit. Shakertown at Pleasant Hill*: Pleasant Hill Press, 1973.

Weiss, Suzanne E., Editor. *Atlas of America. Pleasantville NY*: The Reader's Digest Association, Inc., 2005.

## Interviews

Curry, Larrie. Personal interview. Various dates 2005-06.

Huffman, Dixie. Personal interview. Various dates 2005-06.

## Unpublished Work

East Family Deacons and Deaconesses. *A Temporal Journal Kept by order of the Deacon of the East House, Book B* (Alternatively referred to as the Journal).

Ham, F. Gerald. *Shakerism in the Old West* (Dissertation). University of Kentucky, 1962.

Staff at Pleasant Hill. Notes on the Missionary Journey.

Staff 2 at Pleasant Hill. Biographical Notes Accumulated from Pleasant Hill Family Journals.

# suppliers

**ABRAXAS CROW COMPANY**
Gunter Reimnitz
reimnitz@olypen.com
Port Townsend, WA
360-379-3281
www.abraxascrow.com
*Forge/weld/cut/bend steel sculptures*

**ADAMS & KENNEDY — THE WOOD SOURCE**
6178 Mitch Owen Rd.
P.O. Box 700
Manotick, ON
Canada K4M 1A6
613-822-6800
www.wood-source.com
*Wood supply*

**ADJUSTABLE CLAMP COMPANY**
404 N. Armour St.
Chicago, IL 60622
312-666-0640
www.adjustableclamp.com
*Clamps and woodworking tools*

**AWPA**
American Wood Preservers Association
P.O. Box 361784
Birmingham, AL
205-733-4077
www.awpa.com
*Non-profit organization responsible for promulgating voluntary wood preservation*

**B&Q**
B&Q Head Office
Portswood House
1 Hampshire Corporate Park
Chandlers Ford
Eastleigh
Hampshire SO53 3YX
0845 609 6688
www.diy.com
*Woodworking tools, supplies and hardware*

**BETTER BARNS**
126 Main Street South
Bethlehem, CT 06751
888-266-1960
www.betterbarns.com
*Barns & shed buildings, plans and hardware*

**BUSY BEE TOOLS**
130 Great Gulf Drive
Concord, ON, Canada
L4K 5W1
1-800-461-2879
www.busybeetools.com
*Woodworking tools, supplies and hardware*

**CONSTANTINE'S WOOD CENTER OF FLORIDA**
1040 E. Oakland Park Blvd.
Fort Lauderdale, FL 33334
800-443-9667
www.constantines.com
*Tools, woods, veneers, hardware*

**COTTAGE HOME NETWORK**
Jim Tolpin
www.cottagehome.net
*Cottage homes, the people who build them, and a large collection of resources for further exploration*

**DALY'S**
3525 Stone Way North
Seattle, WA 98103
800-735-7019
www.dalyspaint.com
*Paint, decorating, interior and exterior wood-finishing products*

**DEWALT INDUSTRIAL TOOL COMPANY**
DeWalt Customer Service
626 Hanover Pike
Hamstead, MD 21074
800-4DEWALT
www.dewalt.com
*Industrial and woodworking tools and accessories*

**DOWELMAX**
O.M.S. Company Ltd.
203 - 814 West 15th Street
North Vancouver, B.C.
V7P 1M6 Canada
877-986-9400
www.dowelmax.com
*Precision-engineered dowel joining system*

**EDENSAW WOODS, LTD.**
211 Seton Road
Port Townsend, WA 98368
800-745-3336
www.edensaw.com
*Importers, wholesalers and retailers of domestic and exotic woods, high-quality lumber, plywoods and veneers*

**FESTOOL USA**
Tooltechnic Systems, LLC.
140 Los Carneros Way
Goleta, CA 93117
888-337-8600
www.festoolusa.com
*Woodworking and industrial power tools*

**FRANK PAXTON LUMBER COMPANY**
5701 W. 66th St.
Chicago, IL 60638
800-323-2203
www.paxtonwood.com
*Wood, hardware, tools, books*

**HARDWICK'S**
4214 Roosevelt Way NE
Seattle, WA 98105
866-369-6525
www.ehardwicks.com
*An eclectic family owned and operated hardware and tool store since 1932. The Northwest School of Wooden Boatbuilding takes each entering class on a field trip to Hardwick's to buy their required hand tools*

**THE HOME DEPOT**
2455 Paces Ferry Rd.
Atlanta, GA 30339
800-553-3199 (U.S.)
800-668-0525 (Canada)
www.homedepot.com
*Woodworking tools, supplies and hardware*

**KELLER &. CO.**
1327 I Street
Petaluma, CA 94952
800-995-2456
www.kellerdovetail.com
*The Keller dovetail system offers precision through dovetail router jigs that perform consistently with simplicity, speed and accuracy*

**KREG TOOL COMPANY**
201 Campus Drive
Huxley, IA 50124
800-447-8638
www.kregtool.com
*A pioneer in pocket hole joinery technology and precision measuring accessories for woodworking machinery*

**LEE VALLEY TOOLS LTD.**
P.O. Box 1780
Ogdensburg, NY 13669-6780
800-871-8158 (U.S.)
800-267-8767 (Canada)
www.leevalley.com
*Woodworking tools and hardware*

**LOWE'S HOME IMPROVEMENT WAREHOUSE**
P.O. Box 1111
North Wilkesboro, NC 28656
800-445-6937
www.lowes.com
*Woodworking tools, supplies and hardware*

**MAKITA U.S.A., INC.**
14930 Northam Street
La Mirada, CA 90638
800-4MAKITA
www.makita.com
*Industrial and woodworking tools*

**ROCKLER WOODWORKING AND HARDWARE**
4365 Willow Dr.
Medina, MN 55340
800-279-4441
www.rockler.com
*Woodworking tools, hardware and books*

**THE STANLEY WORKS**
1000 Stanley Drive
New Britain, CT 06053
860-255-5111
www.stanleyworks.com
*Tools and hardware*

**TOOL TREND LTD.**
140 Snow Blvd.
Thornhill, ON
Canada L4K 4L1
416-663-8665
*Woodworking tools and hardware*

**AUGHAN & BUSHNELL MFG. CO.**
11414 Maple Ave.
Hebron, IL 60034
815-648-2446
www.vaughanmfg.com
*Hammers and other tools*

**VINTAGE HARDWARE**
2000 Sims Way
Port Townsend, WA 98368
360-379-9030
www.vintagehardware.com
*Reproduction vintage antique hardware and lighting from the Victorian, Art Nouveau, Art Deco, Bungalow and Mission Style homes*

**VERMONT CASTINGS**
CFM Corporation
2695 Meadowvale Boulevard
Mississauga, Ontario
L5N 8N3 Canada
800-525-1898
www.vermontcastings.com
*Fireplaces, hearths and stoves*

**WOODCRAFT SUPPLY, LLC**
1177 Rosemar Road
P.O. Box 1686
Parkersburg, WV 26102
800-535-4482
www.woodcraft.com
*Woodworking hardware*

**WOODWORKER'S SUPPLY**
1108 North Glenn Rd.
Casper, WY 82601
800-645-9292
www.woodworker.com
*Woodworking tools and accessories, finishing supplies, books and plans*

# index

Aesthetics, 48, 59–60, 68
Authenticity of furniture, 55–56

Banta, Cornelius, 26
Bead
  cock beading, 47, 48
  double-quirked (return), 139
  side bead planes, 47, 98
  Bed with slatted headboard, 122–125
  Blanket chest
  cherry blanket chest, 154–156
  joinery, 58, 60–61, 157
  miniature, 55, 57, 58, 61
  miniature, reproduction, 114–121
  two-drawer, 144–149
Boisseau, Stephen Leonidas, 26
Boxing, 22
Buildings
  disrepair, 32–33
  labor output, 47–48
  structure construction, 20–21
  uses after end of the Shakers, 54–55

Cane Ridge, Kentucky, 14, 16
Centre Family Dwelling, 31, 36–37, 48,
    158–162, 165, 166
Chairs
  counter chair, 130–133
  materials, 21
  post finial, 50
  rockers. See Rockers
  side chairs, 49–50
Chest of drawers
  cupboard over chest of drawers, 46,
    56, 57–58
  joinery, 59
  secretary, 52, 53, 82–93
  simplicity, 47
Cock beading, 47, 48
Communal living, 18
Coopered work, 25
Counter chair, 130–133
Craftsmen, 26–28, 30
Cupboard
  cupboard over chest, 46, 56, 57–58
  hanging, 48, 49, 57, 58–59, 94–99
  red cupboard, 138–143
Curtis, Josephus J., 26

Design features
  cock beading, 47, 48
  construction details, 57–58
  contemporary articulation, 56–57
  country, 45
  curly cherry secretary, 92
  dovetails, 60–61, 118–119, 157
  drawers, 46, 47
  lack of ornamentation, 46, 52
  legs, 48–49, 51, 52
  light and fragile appearance, 48–49
  nails, 58–60, 97
  tops, 46–47, 48–49
  turned feet, 47
  Western, 45
Dovetails, 60–61, 118–119, 157

Drawers. See also Chest of drawers
  decorative bead, 47
  graduated, 46
  secretary, 52, 53, 82–93
  two-drawer blanket chest, 144–149

East Family, 35, 39, 166–167

Feet, 47, 148
Fences, 168
Finials, 50, 63, 68, 108–109
Finish sanding, 121
Front-rung-mortise jig (FRMJ), 110,
    111, 113

Gettys, Leander, 28
Grist mill, 34

Hanger, triple, 99–101
Hardware
  hand-made vs. World production, 21
  on miniature blanket chest, 121
  nails, 58–60, 95
  pocket screws, 59
  secretary drop front, 90
Headstone, 168–169
History of the Shakers
  end of the Shakers, 54–55
  missionary journey, 13–14
  New York City, 12–13
  restoration of Pleasant Hill, 158
  Shawnee Run, 16–18

Insect-repellent herbs, 125
Interpreter's Manual, 39

Joinery
  aesthetics and, 59–60
  blanket chest, 58, 60–61, 157
  counter chair, 133
  curly cherry secretary, 84
  dovetails, 60–61, 118–119, 157
  hanging cupboard, 58–59, 99
  jointing plane, 23
  quality of, 58–59
  on rockers, 70
  Saturday table, 77
Journals, 27, 30
Journeys, 12–15

Kicker strip, 135
Kitchen work table, 55, 150–153

Labor output for building, 47–48
Lathe
  indexing head, 109–110
  sewing rocker back posts, 107–109
  treadle lathe, 22–23
  use of reproduction lathe, 38, 39
Lee, Ann, 12–13, 16
Legs
  examples, 51
  kitchen work table, 153
  Saturday table, 75–76
  side table, 137

square to turned lower section, 52
  thin and light appearance, 48–49
Lids, cupping of, 120–121

Materials
  for chairs, 21
  curly cherry, 83, 85
  hardware. See Hardware
  miniature blanket chest, 117–118
  sewing rocker, 105, 107
  thin and light, 48–49
  wood, 21, 59, 95, 97
Meeting House, 166–167
Metric conversion chart, 5
Millennial Law, 45, 48, 166
Milligan, Alexander, 28
Missionary journey, 13–14
Montfort, Francis, 28
Mortises, 110–113, 120
Mushroom caps, 50, 66, 67, 68

Nails, 58–60, 97
New Light movement, 16–17

Orphans, 37
Oval boxes, 24, 25

Pedestal stands, 52
Pennebaker, William F., 28, 32
Planes
  Banta molder, 22
  bench plane, 98
  collection of, 24
  jointing plane, 23
  molding plane, 26, 97–99
  panel raisers, 23
  plank planes, 20–21
  raising plane, 23
  side-bead plane, 47, 96
  trying plane, 39, 97–99
Plinth, 118–120

Rails, 85, 87
Releasement, 32
Reproductions
  hanging cupboard, 94–99
  miniature blanket chest, 114–120
  Saturday table, 72–77
  sewing rocker, 104–113
  tripod table, 126–129
Restoration of Pleasant Hill
  Centre Family Dwelling, 158–162,
    165, 166
  history of, 158
  rerouting of US 68, 45, 156
  Trustee's Office, 162–165
Rockers
  with arms, 62–69
  mushroom caps, 50, 66, 67, 68
  sewing rocker, 104–113

Safety notice, 4
Sanding, 121
Saturday table, 72–77
Sawmill, 37

Sconce, 76–79
Scratch stock, 47–48, 98
Secretary, 52, 53, 82–93
Sewing desk, 57
Sewing rocker, 104–113
Shawnee Run, 16–18
Shelton, James, 31
Side chairs, 49–50
Side table, 102–103, 134–137
Side-rung-mortise jig (SRMJ), 110, 111
Staveless woodenware, 32
Steam bending, 105
Stickering, 84
Stiles, 84, 86
Suppliers, 175

Tables
  kitchen work table, 55, 148–151
  pedestal stands, 52
  Saturday table, 70–75
  sewing desk, 57
  side table, 100–101, 132–135
  tripod table, 124–127
Tools
  circular saw, 37
  clothes hanger pattern, 24
  drawknife, 25
  front-rung-mortise jig (FRMJ), 110,
    111, 113
  hat shape, 24
  holdfasts, 24
  jointer, 22–23
  lathe. See Lathe
  oval box forms, 24, 25
  paring chisel, 74, 96–97
  planes. See Planes
  side-rung-mortise jig (SRMJ), 112, 113
  stacked molds, 25
  window stay, 24
  woodshops, 19th century, 20–21,
    22–25
  woodshops, modern, 40–43
  workbench, 23
Tops of furniture, 46–47, 48–49
Tripod table, 126–129
Trustee's Office, 162–165

Vases, 66, 68

West Family, 29, 35
Woodshops, 19th century
  blacksmith, 35
  broom shop, 35
  craftsmen, 26–28, 30
  journals, 27, 30
  materials, 21
  structure construction, 20–21
  tools, 20–21, 22–25
  the work, 26
Woodshops, modern
  Interpreter's Manual, 39
  lathe, 38, 39
  tools, 40–43
  visitors, 39
Work, sanctity of, 48